PUFFIN BOOKS
INDIRA GANDHI

A widely travelled freelance writer who enjoys writing on all kinds of topics, Sreelata Menon is a history buff who especially enjoys introducing children to the lives and times of great personalities. Author of *Freelance Writing for the Newbie Writer*, this is her second biography after *Guru Nanak: The Enlightened Master* in the *Puffin Lives* series.

Other books in the *Puffin Lives* series

Mother Teresa: Apostle of Love
by Rukmini Chawla
Jawaharlal Nehru: The Jewel of India
by Aditi De
Ashoka: the Great and Compassionate King
by Subhadra Sen Gupta
Rani Lakhsmibai: The Valiant Queen of Jhansi
by Deepa Agarwal
Akbar: The Mighty Emperor
by Kavitha Mandana
Mahatma Gandhi: The Father of the Nation
by Subhadra Sen Gupta
The 14th Dalai Lama: Buddha of Compassion
by Aravinda Anantharaman
Swami Vivekananda: A Man with a Vision
by Devika Rangachari
Gautama Buddha: The Lord of Wisdom
by Rohini Chowdhury
Guru Nanak: The Enlightened Master
by Sreelata Menon
Chanakya: The Master of Statecraft
by Deepa Agarwal

INDIRA
Gandhi
CHILD OF POLITICS

SREELATA MENON

PUFFIN BOOKS

PUFFIN BOOKS
Published by the Penguin Group
Penguin Books India Pvt. Ltd, 11 Community Centre, Panchsheel Park,
New Delhi 110 017, India
Penguin Group (USA) Inc., 375 Hudson Street, New York, New York 10014,
USA
Penguin Group (Canada), 90 Eglinton Avenue East, Suite 700, Toronto,
Ontario, M4P 2Y3, Canada (a division of Pearson Penguin Canada Inc.)
Penguin Books Ltd, 80 Strand, London WC2R 0RL, England
Penguin Ireland, 25 St Stephen's Green, Dublin 2, Ireland
(a division of Penguin Books Ltd)
Penguin Group (Australia), 707 Collins Street, Melbourne, Victoria 3008,
Australia (a division of Pearson Australia Group Pty Ltd)
Penguin Group (NZ), 67 Apollo Drive, Rosedale, Auckland 0632,
New Zealand (a division of Pearson New Zealand Ltd)
Penguin Books (South Africa) (Pty) Ltd, Block D, Rosebank Office Park,
181 Jan Smuts Avenue, Parktown North, Johannesburg 2193, South Africa

Penguin Books Ltd, Registered Offices: 80 Strand, London WC2R 0RL,
England

First published in Puffin by Penguin Books India 2013

Copyright © Sreelata Menon 2013

All rights reserved

10 9 8 7 6 5 4 3 2 1

ISBN 9780143332237

Typeset in Bembo by Eleven Arts, Delhi
Printed at Replika Press Pvt. Ltd, India

Contents

CHAPTER ONE

An Assassination Most Foul   **1**

CHAPTER TWO

Revenge Served Cold   **6**

CHAPTER THREE

Where It All began . . .   **12**

CHAPTER FOUR

Political Baptism   **19**

CHAPTER FIVE

Home Alone   **26**

CHAPTER SIX

A New World   **31**

CHAPTER SEVEN

Another World   **37**

CHAPTER EIGHT

Mummie's Best Friend   **42**

CHAPTER NINE

A Changing World   **48**

CHAPTER TEN

Her Dadu and Her Papu   **53**

CHAPTER ELEVEN
Politics in Her Blood   **59**

CHAPTER TWELVE
Family Ties   **65**

CHAPTER THIRTEEN
Teen Murti House   **72**

CHAPTER FOURTEEN
Finding Her Feet   **77**

CHAPTER FIFTEEN
It's a Girl   **83**

CHAPTER SIXTEEN
Not a Smooth Ride   **90**

CHAPTER SEVENTEEN
A Feisty Leader   **96**

CHAPTER EIGHTEEN
A Basketful of Woes   **102**

CHAPTER NINETEEN
Mixed Fortunes   **109**

CHAPTER TWENTY
The Curtain Comes Down   **115**

CHAPTER TWENTY-ONE
Yet It Was Not Always Politics   **120**

Trivia Treasury   **127**

1   An Assassination Most Foul

It was a lovely morning. A lingering aroma of smoking twigs and burnt leaves hung in the cool, dry air. Bathed in the October sun Delhi was at her autumnal best and 1 Safdarjang Road, the official residence of India's prime minister Indira Gandhi, was slowly waking up to another ordinarily busy day.

A modest house with neatly laid gardens, 1 Safdarjang Road was home to not only Mrs Gandhi but also her eldest son Rajiv, his wife Sonia and their two children—fourteen-year-old Rahul and Priyanka who was just twelve. As sparrows hopped around noisily among the flowering bushes in the garden and koels frolicked merrily on its lawns, it did appear that morning that god was indeed in his heaven and all was right with the world.

'How are you? Were you hurt?' asked Mrs Gandhi in some concern as she walked into the room where her grandchildren, getting ready for school, were already at breakfast. 'You are back!' they chorused in delighted surprise. Their father they knew was away in West Bengal and their grandmother was supposed to have been in Bhubaneswar. 'Yes,' she nodded. 'But I was told about the accident. Were you hurt?' She asked again. Always busy and constantly on the move, Mrs Gandhi had very little time to spend at home. After all being the prime minister of a country was no easy task. Yet she somehow always managed to make time for Rahul and Priyanka.

She had in fact, a few days ago, taken them for a fleeting but super holiday to Srinagar. They had stayed at the panoramic Chasma Shahi guest house and gone shopping at the Srinagar market as well. Then with hardly a day's break between trekking up the Sankaracharya Hill, near the famous Dal Lake and dropping them off in Delhi, she had dashed off again on a strenuous election tour of Orissa.

But now as they helped themselves to some orange juice with eggs, cereal and toast the children realized that she had cut short her trip because of their accident the day before. A van had jumped the lights and collided with their escort car. 'We are all right,' they assured her earnestly, anxious to set her mind at ease.

Rahul and Priyanka adored their grandmother and she in turn doted on them. Mrs Gandhi was not only warm and loving, she was great fun to be with as well. She was also a marvellous fund of exciting stories. She knew a whole host of stuff other grown-ups weren't interested in. She even knew, as Priyanka says 'all about the swirls and textures in a pebble and the myriad colours of a beetle's wing,' and even a walk in the garden with her was an 'adventure and an exploration.' (*Letters from a Father to His Daughter*, Jawaharlal Nehru) Mealtimes in particular were fun times when she would often tell them fascinating stories that she herself had heard from her father. Yes, as far as they were concerned, she was the best grandmother in the world!

But that day she was on an extremely busy schedule. So having satisfied herself that the children were fine she went into her study to look through some urgent files. However, just before they left for school she called them back for another hug and a kiss. A few minutes later, a little after nine, she was ready to set out for her office on Akbar Road next door, just across the garden.

Clad in a cheerful orange sari Mrs Gandhi came out of her house and nimbly strode down the path through her garden towards the wicket gate that led to her office. She was scheduled to meet a British television crew who were apparently all ready and waiting. Her usual retinue, a personal staff that included five security men, followed her. Despite having gone to bed well past midnight and up at six to breakfast with the children, she was in unusually high spirits. She was probably relieved that Rahul and Priyanka were unharmed and that the accident was not as bad as she had feared.

As she approached the wicket gate she spotted Beant Singh, one of her favourite bodyguards. He was a Sikh policeman and had been part of her security for years. He seemed to be attentively standing by to open the gate. She smiled and nodded a greeting to him. But as she drew near, Beant Singh suddenly pulled out his .38mm service revolver. 'What are you doing?' cried Mrs Gandhi in surprise. In reply Beant Singh simply raised his arm and shot her straight in the abdomen. In dazed incredulity she tried to shield herself while he fired at her again and again. Four times did he shoot her at point-blank range. As she crumbled to the ground another young khaki-clad guard, Satwant Singh who had been lurking behind a hedge, came up. He brutally let loose a further thirty rounds from his own Sten gun, peppering her already stricken body with more bullets. The impact almost lifted Mrs Gandhi's frail body off the ground and spun it around violently before bringing it crashing down again. And sadly in a matter of seconds, one of India's most charismatic leaders lay dying in her own garden shot by her own bodyguards. It was the 31st of October and the year 1984. She was a few days short of her sixty-seventh birthday.

Why had she been so cruelly assassinated? Why had bodyguards who were trusted to protect her with their own lives taken hers?

Delhi

Over centuries the city of Delhi has played an important role in every empire that has sprung up around it. From 1206–1526 it was the capital of the Delhi Sultanate and then continued to be an important city during the early Mughal rule. In 1639, Shah Jahan created Shahjahanabad to the north of the earlier settlements of Delhi and made that the capital of the Mughal Empire. In 1857 the British defeated the then emperor Bahadur Shah Zafar and brought an end to the Mughal era. The British continued to rule India from Calcutta till 1911, when they decided to shift their capital to Delhi. King George V and Queen Mary laid the foundation for New Delhi, south-west of Shahjahanabad. Designed and built by Edwin Lutyens and Herbert Baker, the contractor for the project was Sir Sobha Singh (famous journalist Khushwant Singh's father). Construction started in 1918 and took about thirteen years to complete. It was named 'New Delhi' in 1927 and inaugurated in 1931. When India became independent in 1947, New Delhi remained the capital and continues to do so till today.

2 Revenge Served Cold

Indira Gandhi was not only one of India's longest-serving prime ministers, she was also someone who was deeply loved by the masses. So why had she been so violently killed?

The reason was not too difficult to find. When Beant Singh first opened fire, the entourage accompanying her was for a moment shocked into immobility. While the others dived to the ground, only Sub-inspector Rameshwar Dayal was quick to react. He lunged forward but was at once brought down by a bullet in the thigh. As Mrs Gandhi's security guards tried in stunned disbelief to gather their stupefied wits, the killers themselves laid down their weapons and stood quietly by her limp body. Then, when they belatedly pounced on him, Beant Singh—not a whit perturbed by his dastardly crime—told them, 'We have done what we had to do; now you can do what you have to.' It was an apparent reference to Operation Blue Star, the military action Indira Gandhi had ordered a few months ago.

When India became independent in 1947 and was partitioned into India and Pakistan, the Sikhs too had asked for an independent homeland. This was not granted. So even after independence some Sikhs continued to propagate the idea of a separate Khalistan (The Land of the Pure). The movement began to gather steam under a certain Jagjit Singh Chohan. Soon with Sant Jarnail Singh Bhindranwale, who became the face of the Sikh separatist movement in India, it turned extremely militant. And to achieve their objective the militants started to heap atrocities on the police, non-Sikhs and moderate Sikhs.

When Bhindranwale began a massive fortification of the Golden Temple in Amritsar by amassing men and weapons inside, Indira Gandhi on the 5 June 1984 as the prime minister of India sanctioned military action. She ordered the army to storm the Golden Temple and flush out the heavily-armed militants holed up inside. Termed 'Operation Bluestar' it succeeded in eliminating the militants. But it also caused the death of many army men and hundreds of innocent pilgrims as well. The centuries-old sacred shrine of the Sikhs, the holy Akal Takht, was also more than partially destroyed.

Although it was quickly rebuilt, the Sikhs could neither accept nor forgive the fact that the temple had been damaged or that the army had been sent into its premises. There was widespread criticism at the timing and even whether such an action was required at all. Overnight Mrs Gandhi became a much-hated figure among the Sikh community. Her life was said to be in danger ever since.

Fearing just such a backlash, her chief of security and other officials had pleaded with her to replace all her Sikh bodyguards. They had in fact wanted to transfer Beant Singh out. But Mrs Gandhi had refused. She was not willing to believe that she had anything to fear from the Sikhs, least of all from Beant Singh who had been with her for so long. But Beant Singh and Satwant Singh had been extremely angered and agitated by the damage done to the Akal Takht. They held Mrs Gandhi solely responsible for its desecration. So they quietly bided their time. They plotted and planned and when the time was ripe, struck. To avenge the storming of the Golden Temple, they riddled with bullets a person who was not only an unarmed woman but one whom as prime minister, they were sworn to serve, protect and defend. As for Indira Gandhi, it was a critical political decision that boomeranged fatally.

Now hearing the gunfire Sonia rushed out of the house. Dashing across the lawn she found her mother-in-law lying in a pool of blood. And while the assassins, who had made no attempt to escape, were marched away to the guardroom, a distraught Sonia gathered the shattered body in her arms and with the other aides took Mrs Gandhi to hospital. Pandemonium broke out when the medical staff realized who it was that had been brought in. Panic-stricken doctors rushed to attend on her, but it was too late. It is believed that the prime minister was already dead before she hit the ground, because in a matter of minutes some thirty odd bullets had been pumped into her small, delicate frame. Yet anxious doctors worked hard for hours to try and revive her. But to no avail.

Five long hours after she was first shot, Indira Gandhi was officially declared dead. A stunned nation was informed that their leader was no more. 'I don't mind if my life goes in the service of the nation. If I die today every drop of my blood will invigorate the nation,' she had told a mammoth crowd in Bhubaneswar just the day before. Now to the country and its people her words seemed prophetic.

If you think the violence ended there, you are mistaken. After the two assassins were led away to the guardhouse by the Indo-Tibetan police on duty, there was in the space of a few minutes a further volley of gunfire from within. Beant Singh had apparently lunged for a weapon in an attempt to escape. He was shot at and died instantly. Satwant Singh similarly was shot but survived with serious injuries. He was arrested and taken away.

Now Beant Singh and Satwant Singh had no doubt accomplished their objective and punished the prime minister with her life, but what they also provoked was a reprisal of enormous proportions. Their act unleashed a carnage against the Sikhs that was reminiscent of the days of the Partition of India. Rampaging mobs took to the streets and for three whole days Sikh men, women and children were remorselessly slaughtered in Delhi. They were pulled out of their homes and vehicles, and systematically knifed or set on fire. Trains to and fro from Punjab became burning torches. Anyone in a turban was fair game. In what has now come to be known as the horrendous 1984 anti-Sikh riots the Sikh community probably had to pay a price more terrible than Operation Blue Star that had started it all.

Indira Gandhi was not only the daughter of Jawaharlal Nehru, India's first prime minister, she was also a dynamic leader in her own right. She may have been hated by some but she was also genuinely loved without exception by a majority of the Indian people. Her entire life ever since she was a little girl, she once said, had revolved round India and her people. There was never a time when politics did not play a part in her life. Now the question is how did Indira Gandhi's life become so inextricably linked with the politics of her country that it even became the very reason for her death?

To find out we need to go back to the beginning . . .

The Partition
Britain had been trading in India since the 17th century. Over the years the British gradually consolidated and expanded militarily and administratively and then ruled India for the next two hundred years. At midnight on the 14th of August 1947 India attained her independence, though not before she was partitioned into two countries. A day earlier, Muslim majority areas of the Punjab and Bengal had become a new nation—Pakistan. But when the border was drawn through the Punjab and Bengal, Hindus and Muslims belonging to both parts tried to or were forced to jump sides. Horrific riots broke out.

Friends turned on friends, neighbours killed neighbours and refugee-filled trains with murdered Hindus and slain Muslims criss-crossed the new borders. Millions were killed and even more were displaced. Thus amidst the terrible bloodshed of the Partition were born the new Islamic Republic of Pakistan and the secular Republic of India.

3 Where It All Began . . .

Allahabad
19 November 1917

Young Kamala Nehru was in pain. She hadn't realized that having a baby would be so difficult. She should customarily have had her baby in the comfort of her own father's home in Delhi. But her father-in-law Motilal Nehru, who was extremely fond of her, had decreed otherwise. His son Jawaharlal's child had to be born in his house attended to by the best doctors in the country. And so it had come to pass. Now there she was in a sterile room in Anand Bhawan surrounded by doctors and nurses, while everyone was gathered outside, waiting.

It was a dark and stormy night. It was cold too, but the home of the Nehrus was ablaze with lights and bustling with activity. A palatial house by any standards, Anand Bhawan had forty-two exquisitely furnished rooms built around a large courtyard with verandas and swimming pools. Built on the lines of a stately British country house, it was situated in the Civil Lines area of Allahabad and a stone's throw from the River Ganges. Its gardens always abloom with lovely flowers and fruits were during the day a profusion of colour.

The family loved to ride and adored animals. So its sprawling grounds had several stables and kennels that housed as many as twenty-two horses and sixteen dogs. More than a hundred attendants lived on the estate as well. Whenever the family entertained, the house came alive with its brilliant chandeliers and Bohemian crystals. With its elegant British crockery, Persian carpets and Kashmiri silk durries, Anand Bhawan was an opulent mix of European and Indian influences. Motilal Nehru used the part of the house that was completely westernized while his wife Swaroop Rani occupied a section that was Indian in every way. It was for all its grandeur a happy house that echoed with its owner's exuberance. It was aptly named Anand Bhawan.

And now across its large central courtyard, where the family generally gathered to sit around, was for the moment where the action was. While Motilal Nehru kept pacing up and down, others were huddled in little groups chatting or sipping at their drinks. Yet despite the party atmosphere there was an air of watchful expectancy tinged with anxiety. Jawaharlal was also among those who had gathered there. So were his two sisters. While fifteen-year-old Sarup was allowed to linger, Krishna, who was just ten, had been sent up to bed by her governess. But she had managed to sneak back to see what was happening. Jawaharlal kept glancing every now and then at the door across the yard. So little Krishna knew that her favourite person, Jawaharlal's wife Kamala, was behind that door in the labour room about to have her baby and her brother was just as nervous as anyone else.

About an hour before midnight the door suddenly opened and the Scottish doctor attending on Kamala came out. 'It's a bonnie lassie,' he announced cheerfully. A tired Kamala, now cuddling her newborn, could hear Jawaharlal's mother confirming the news to the others. But was there a touch of disappointment in her voice? Like many conservative north Indian mothers she had perhaps hoped for a grandson. But Motilal Nehru on the other hand, Kamala could tell, was thrilled. He had anyway been delighted at the prospect of a grandchild. 'She may prove to be better than a thousand sons,' he told his wife. He could not have foreseen the truth of his words. As for Jawaharlal it didn't matter either way. He was quietly happy as was his wife that they now had a little baby who was so adorable. She was a dear little thing with masses of black hair and enormously large eyes. To her young parents she was 'Priyadarshini', meaning 'dear to the sight, or 'dear to behold'. With 'Indira' from 'Indirani' after her paternal great grandmother's name tagged on before 'Priyadarshini', she officially became 'Indira Priyadarshini', otherwise affectionately known as 'Indu' to those near and dear.

Indira Priyadarshini soon endeared herself to everyone. She could not but be loved and doted upon considering the genes she carried. Her mother was a delicate shimmering beauty and her father was a handsome intellectual. Her grandparents on both sides were affluent, cultured and distinguished people. While her paternal grandfather Motilal Nehru was a brilliant lawyer making oodles of money and living in style, her maternal grandfather Jawaharmul Kaul was also no less a prominent personage in Delhi. He was a highly respected businessman and his wife Rajpati was just as lovely as her daughter Kamala.

Actually the Nehrus were also from Delhi. They were in fact Kauls too. They were Kashmiri Brahmins who had left Kashmir to settle in Delhi in the 18th century. And since in Delhi they lived next to a canal called 'nehar' in Urdu, they began to be referred to as Kaul-Nehru, as in 'those (Kauls) living by the canal'. With time the Kaul got dropped and only the Nehru remained. Then during the upheaval of the Sepoy Mutiny in 1857 the family moved to Agra. It was in Agra that Motilal Nehru was born and lived awhile with his mother and elder brothers, one of whom became a lawyer. When the law courts shifted to Allahabad so did the family. But by that time Motilal too had taken up law. He soon began to make a name for himself as a brilliant barrister. Now Anand Bhawan where he lived was not only home to his own family but also to his brother's family and other assorted relatives.

While the Nehrus in Allahabad were rejoicing over the latest addition to their family, the rest of the world was at war. The immediate cause for the First World War that started in 1914 was the assassination of Archduke Ferdinand of Austria-Hungary by a Serb. So Austria-Hungary declared war on Serbia. When that happened, Russia, which had a defence alliance with

Serbia came to her help. In retaliation Germany, who, a defence pact with Austria-Hungary, declared war on Russia. Now all the other countries of the world which had similar pacts with each other swung into action aligning themselves on their respective sides. The Allies (Russia, Britain, France, Belgium, Japan, Italy and the US) finally prevailed and the Austria-Hungary-Germany combine was defeated. The war ended in 1918 with the Treaty of Versailles (France) but not before killing some eight million people and wounding more than thirty million. It was a pointless tragedy that saw for the first time the use of machine guns, tanks and poison gas besides introducing a new kind of aerial warfare.

The war also set the Bolsheviks (peasants) on a rampage in Russia in the very month that Indira was born. It eventually led to the brutal overthrow of the monarchy in what is known as the Russian Revolution of 1917. Elsewhere in India too, though the struggle for independence had not actually begun, the rumblings had already started. The Indian National Congress which had been founded by Allan Hume in 1885 as a debating club for westernized Indians was now beginning to voice nationalistic aspirations, and a certain Mohandas Karamchand Gandhi was beginning to take an active interest in Indian politics.

Allahabad

Allahabad, one of the oldest cities in India, is among the main pilgrim centres of the Hindus. Lord Brahma, it is said, offered his first sacrifice here after creating the world. It was known as as Prayag (place of sacrifice) till the Mughals renamed it Allahabad (the abode of god). It has the Triveni Sangam (confluence of the three rivers—Ganga, Yamuna and the mythical Saraswati) where Hindus come to immerse the ashes of their dead and take a dip to wash away their sins. Millions of pilgrims throng Allahabad also for a ritualistic dip during the Kumbha Melas. Emperor Akbar's magnificent fort near the Sangam which later housed British garrisons serves the Indian army even today. The British East India Company handed over control of India to the British Crown here and it is famous for the role it played during India's struggle for independence. Often referred to as the Oxford of the East, Allahabad is today a part of the state of Uttar Pradesh.

The Sepoy Mutiny

In 1857 the British East India Company introduced a breech loading Enfield rifle for its Indian troops (sepoys). The new rifle had a greased cartridge that required to be bitten off before loading. Now the Hindu sepoys to whom cows were sacred feared it was the fat of the cow. The Muslim sepoys who considered pigs anti-Islam believed the grease was the fat from pork. So both were aggrieved and they revolted against the British. The first uprising took place at the Meerut Garrison and it spread to Delhi where the sepoys declared Bahadur Shah Zafar, the weak and aging Mughal Emperor, as their commander. The plunder and massacre that followed left Delhi in ruins. Other centres across the country soon joined the rebellion. The British acted swiftly. Bahadur Shah Zafar was defeated and exiled to Burma and every suspected mutineer was hunted down and brutally killed. The mutiny was snuffed out. But it sent a strong message to the British that the Indians could no longer be taken for granted. The East India Company's reign in India too came to an end as control was now handed over to the British Crown. This mutiny is generally considered to be the first battle in India's struggle for independence.

4   Political Baptism

The nationalistic rumblings gradually grew louder and by the time little Indira was two years old, the nation was at loggerheads with its British rulers.

The Indian National Congress had supported Britain in the war. As a reward for their support, the Congress, of which Motilal Nehru was a member, hoped for the kind of self-government that other British colonies like Canada and Australia enjoyed. These countries ruled themselves even while remaining a part of the British Empire. But to their disappointment India received instead the tyrannical Rowlatt Act of 1919. This act took away all civil rights of the people and gave the police unlimited powers to take any action against them as and when they wished. Congress was both dismayed and agitated. And soon an upheaval of gigantic proportions took place.

The trigger was a barrister named Mohandas Karamchand Gandhi fresh from South Africa. He set in motion a novel form of protest. It was called 'satyagraha'—satyam for truth and agraha for insistence or force—'Truth Force'. A Sanskrit word, satyagraha broadly means to protest peacefully for truth. Gandhiji told people 'violence only provokes violence so if you protest against all injustice peacefully and non-violently, guns and knives will not be required to start or continue a revolution.' He was right. What could the police do if multitudes of people simply came out on to the street to protest and did not retaliate or fight back even when beaten up? They could only be arrested.

So now he appealed to people across the country to join him in a civil disobedience movement for the abolition of the Rowlatt Act and to court arrest. Jawaharlal Nehru, who had already begun dabbling in politics, was immediately attracted to this movement. But unfortunately his law-abiding father Motilal Nehru was not impressed. 'What good would people breaking the law and going to jail achieve?' he asked. Arguments between father and son arose and tempers flared. Although her mother Kamala tried hard to keep the peace, little Indira could sense the tension between her Dadu and her Papu. But Jawaharlal remained determined to join the movement. So Motilal Nehru decided to invite Gandhiji himself to Anand Bhawan for discussions. This marks the Nehru family's involvement with Indian politics. Soon Gandhiji became a motivating influence in all their lives including little Indira's. However, this visit was soon followed by an incident that completely changed all equations.

The response to Gandhiji's call for a hartal or non-violent strike was immediate. All over the country offices, schools and colleges closed down and peaceful protest marches were organized. Unfortunately, violence broke out in the Punjab. So the British banned all public gatherings. However, on 13 April 1919, when thousands of unarmed men, women and children gathered peacefully to celebrate Baisakhi in Jallianwala Bagh in Amritsar, they were ruthlessly gunned down. Now known as the Jallianwala Bagh massacre, this bloodbath changed forever the attitude of all Indians, rich and poor, towards the British.

It also changed Motilal Nehru dramatically. He gave up his successful practice overnight and joined his son and Gandhiji. So did the entire Congress. The civil disobedience movement began to instantly gather momentum and 'satyagraha' started to gain steam. Non-cooperation became the new mantra of the people and jails their new homes. Soon came the call to boycott not only all 'Made in England' goods but all foreign products. The Nehru family led by example.

Little Indu was excited. She had heard there was going to be a bonfire on the terrace. But her parents had sent her to bed. 'Please let me stay, Dadu,' she begged her grandfather. And so she remained. But now as the flames rose high in the sky she rubbed her eyes in disbelief. Instead of dead twigs and dry leaves, going up in smoke were expensive British suits and elegant foreign shirts. They belonged to her grandfather and father. Soon her mother's brocades and exquisite French chiffons joined the burning pile. So did her grandmother's imported linen and her aunts' lovely western outfits. Indira watched in dismay as they quickly turned to black soot. She was too small to understand why, but she was not too young to comprehend that something momentous and significant was happening. And it was. The bonfire was symbolic of the massive anti-British movement that was making waves all across the country.

Like the rest of the country, not only Indira's father but also her grandfather now began to seek arrest. Motilal Nehru was soon arrested for organizing a peaceful hartal against a British royal visit. They came to Anand Bhawan to take him away. It was four-year-old Indira's first brush with the police. She accompanied her mother to court where her grandfather was being tried. Naturally it was her first experience of a courtroom too. The moment she saw her grandfather she ran up to him. There was pin drop silence as Motilal Nehru, with a solemn Indira sitting on his lap, refused to defend himself against the trumped up charges. Her large eyes filled with unshed tears as her Dadu was pulled away and taken to prison.

Indu herself was soon put to the test. A friend of her mother's came calling one day and she gave Indira a lovely frock from France. Wouldn't you as a little girl or boy be thrilled if anyone brought you a gift, especially from abroad? So was Indira and everyone could see how enchanted she was by the outfit. But her mother quietly reminded her of the bonfire. Indira looked at the gift longingly, then saying, 'No thank you', returned it politely.

'What about your doll?' the lady then asked her. 'Isn't that foreign too?' Poor Indira didn't know what to do. She looked at her mother mutinously. The doll was her best friend. How could she give it away?

She didn't do anything right then. But one morning after moping around the house for days, she went up to the terrace with her doll. Unhappiness writ large on her face she slowly lit a match to it, just like she had seen the bonfire lit. Heartbroken, she was ill for many days after this. But she too had to do her bit for the country whatever the cost, didn't she? Just like everyone else? In hindsight this was probably her moment of political baptism.

As they grew more and more involved in their country's fortunes, the luxurious lifestyle of the Nehrus gradually changed. Their wealth too began to be diverted to the cause. All the lavishness and splendour that Anand Bhawan was known for now gave way to a much more austere way of living. The parties stopped. So did the wine and the merrymaking. Frugal fare and homespun khadi replaced elaborate meals and expensive silks. The men in the Nehru family were more in jail than at home. If neither, they would be out on the streets protesting. And when they refused to pay the petty fines levied on them, the police would land up at any hour of the day to take away their expensive carpets and furniture. Boisterous and high-spirited as most little girls are, Indira often flew at them in rage. 'They are ours,' she would shout in her childish voice, 'you can't take them away.' Once she almost sliced an officer's fingers off with a bread knife. They now began to live, as her aunt Krishna said, from moment to moment: a rather confused and unpredictable life, never knowing what would happen next.

Bapu

Affectionately known as 'Bapu', Mohandas Karamchand Gandhi is considered to be the 'Father of the Nation'. He was born in Porbander, Gujarat in 1869 and studied law at University College, London. He came back to India in 1915 after twenty-two years in South Africa where he had protested strongly against the apartheid system—a racist form of governance where the 'whites' treated the blacks as well as Indians as slaves. In the process Gandhiji evolved 'satyagraha', a new method of peaceful protest.

Gandhiji used satyagraha effectively in India as well. His first success was in Champaran where he championed the cause of the poor indigo farmers. He mobilized them in a peaceful mass movement against the British till they were allowed to grow whatever crop they wished instead of the indigo dye that Britain wanted. After that every repressive act of the British was met with the same kind of protests.

Soon to be known as the Mahatma he appealed to people across the country to disobey and not cooperate with the authorities by peacefully and non-violently putting down their tools, stopping work and coming out on the streets to protest and boycott the British. But the situation would at times turn aggressive. Gandhiji would then go on fasts to stop the violence. Despite being jailed regularly he galvanized people with his 'fasts' and used his hunger strikes as a weapon to dictate terms to the British. When the British levied a tax on salt, he marched 241 miles to Dandi to produce his own salt from the sea and was jailed along with some 60,000 people across the country. He also encouraged the women of India to come out on peaceful pickets and led by his wife Kasturba, they were often jailed as well. He advocated 'ahimsa' or non-violence at all costs and tried to improve the status of the lower castes. He also made the charkha a national symbol and khadi a clothing of pride to replace foreign clothes.

In his trademark loincloth, dhoti and stick he held his own wherever he went in London or in his ashrams at Sabarmati and Wardha. While 'Purna Swaraj' or complete independence was declared in 1929, he launched the Quit India Movement in 1942. It broke his heart when on gaining independence in 1947, India was partitioned and Pakistan was created. Refusing to become the prime minister, Gandhiji, even as riots broke out, continued to fight for Hindu-Muslim amity. On 30 January 1948 at his prayer meeting in Delhi, he was shot dead by a Hindu fanatic Nathuram Godse who believed Gandhiji's ideas were anti-Hindu.

5   Home Alone

Little Indu now found life extremely muddling. She didn't know when she would see her father or grandfather or for how long. 'Was jail their second home?' she began to wonder. Wasn't she always seeing them off to prison or visiting them there? And when some of her parents' friends dropped by one day she told them in all earnestness, 'Nobody's at home. They have all gone out to jail,' as if it was the most normal thing to do. But, 'It's just not fair,' little Indira would often mutter to herself.

Why, even her mother was busy these days. The civil disobedience movement was gathering steam and with most of their men behind bars, the women were also out organizing mass protests. Leading from the front were as usual the Nehru ladies. And to Indira's dismay Kamala too was more out of the house than in.

Imagine yourself in Indira's place. Wouldn't you resent it if your parents were carted off by the police every now and then? Similarly Indira did so. But since she knew no other kind of life she knew no better than to complain.

Life was so much more fun when her parents were home, like now. 'Run on your toes Indu, not on your heels. Let your heels breathe,' her father exhorted her. And when she slowed down, 'No not like that, throw yourself forward like an athlete, like this' he said, showing her how to do it. The excited hustle and bustle in the early hours of the morning had told Indira that her father was home. And even as she quickly jumped out of bed and ran to get ready, she knew her Papu would soon come looking for her as he always tried to make the most of their time together. And so he had. He was now teaching her to run fast elegantly and stylishly.

He was also keen that she learnt to ride and swim. So if she was not poring over books with him or walking hand in hand discussing the world, she was riding, swimming or running, till she was doing all three gracefully and in perfect coordination of mind and body. And she treasured these moments with him.

Her father when away also wrote often to his 'Priyadarshini—dear to the sight but dearer still when sight is denied'. He constantly urged her to take care of her health and also to go visit him in prison. Her grandfather too, when home, indulged her every whim. And as for her mother, she was as always, her best friend. All the same Indira wished they wouldn't go away so often.

But it wasn't as if there was no one else to care for her. In fact there was a houseful of other people. Her grandmother like all grandmothers loved her dearly. She often on the sly gave her sweets from her doli—a metal ringed cupboard. And Indira, identifying her with the cupboard, even took to calling her 'Dol-amma' instead of the usual 'Dadi'. Her aunt Krishna, more like an elder sister than an aunt, also adored her immensely. Even her grandmother's sister 'Bibi amma', stern as she always was, told her exciting bedtime stories. And then there were her maternal grandparents in Delhi. They pampered and spoilt her silly. In reality, apart from her parents, who were forever trying to discipline her, almost everyone including the servants indulged her.

But for all that Indira still felt lonely. Everyone was busy and so caught up in their own activities that there was no one actually in charge of her or with her even when her parents were around. She had no fixed meal or bed timings or any kind of proper routine, and since she was so often schooled at home she kept no regular study hours either. There was also nobody really to play with or even talk to for days on end. So more often than not even while the house was spilling over with people, she was usually left to her own devices or to fend for herself.

She had a free run of the house and its large garden. When not in her room, she was either up a tree or behind one, cleverly devising her own games. 'Indu, Induuu,' Indira often heard them call. It was probably past lunchtime or time for tea. She could hike up a tree better than most boys. Then hidden among the leaves and engrossed in the folk tales of Rajasthan or the antics of ancient heroes, she would wait to be discovered. She took great delight in doing this. She frequently fooled her grandmother's servants into believing she was in her room—even at night—when she was actually outside, listening to the call of the birds or contemplating the wonders of the sky.

And she loved her Dadu's vast library. *Alice in Wonderland* was one of her favourite books. The fairy tales and stories from around the world were so thrilling. They transported her to exciting new worlds of valour and heroism. They were better than any friend. However, even if you are good at making up your own games, like she was or loved reading as she did, how long can you play on own or even get lost in fantasy?

So it was actually an abnormal and unsettled life and she grew up not quite neglected but generally alone and insecure with no friends her age.

With the struggle for India's independence gaining ground the Nehru household soon became the hub of various political activities. Renaming it Swaraj Bhawan, Motilal Nehru even gave Anand Bhawan away to the Congress to house its offices. He built another smaller home for himself within its compound but big it still was. This became the new Anand Bhawan and Indira grew up right in the midst of all this hectic political activity. Unlike the rest of her family who had known luxury, Indira, a victim of her circumstances, was growing up mostly alone in an atmosphere of austerity and political sacrifice.

And when in the midst of all the political turmoil her mother fell ill, she was left even more on her own. Just after she had given birth to a baby boy who died within a few days of his birth, Kamala who was never really been of robust health now became extremely unwell with Tuberculosis (TB). The baby's death devastated the entire family including seven-year-old Indira who had been so looking forward to a younger brother. But what was more devastating for the little girl was that she was not allowed to be with her mother who was now confined to a Lucknow hospital. Bereft of her mother's company she felt lonelier than ever before. TB, a lingering disease of the lungs, though today is completely curable, was in those days almost like a death knell and considered contagious.

Behind Bars

During the satyagraha, civil disobedience and non-cooperation movements, civilian protesters were regularly jailed for breaking the law. By putting them behind bars the British hoped to nip the protests immediately or break them up quickly. These jails were usually converted sheds, stonewalled barracks or forts where they were often packed almost fifty to a shed. At times open to the skies but more often than not small and claustrophobic, these cells were rat infested, dirty and disease prone. Jawaharlal Nehru even fell dangerously ill with Typhus once while in prison. As the protests gathered momentum jails sprung up all over the country. From Naini-Allahabad, Almora-Nainital, Alipore-Calcutta, Sabarmati-Ahmedabad, Yerawada-Poona, Lucknow, Bareilly, Dehradun, to Bombay and Ahmadnagar, Jawaharlal Nehru and Gandhiji were imprisoned in most of them.

A New World

Jawaharlal Nehru was furious. He was away in prison again and his father was being unreasonable. How could he send Indu to St Cecilia's? Didn't Motilal Nehru know it was a school run by three British sisters? Wasn't it against the spirit of the civil disobedience movement and the boycott of 'everything British'? But an unconvinced Motilal Nehru refused to pull her out. Indira, he felt, would get the kind of quality education there that her aunts had received. He was not overly concerned about the political aspect as Indira had already had a rather brief but unimpressive spell in a kindergarten in Delhi and the Modern School in Allahabad, a nationalist institution. But a determined anti-British Jawaharlal wanted her out.

A fierce argument raged between father and son. With both sticking to their stands Gandhiji was called upon to play mediator. Motilal Nehru finally gave in and Indira, it was decided, would be taught at home by tutors. The little girl was overjoyed. She hadn't liked the school one bit. Her khadi dress and her lonely nature had made her an oddity there and she had been miserable. But now began Indira's rather erratic academic life. This was also about the time that her mother had lost the baby and been diagnosed with TB. It was hence decided that Kamala should go to Switzerland for medical treatment.

So the young Nehrus set sail for Europe. On reaching Geneva, Indira enrolled in the L'Ecole Internationale, a day school run by the League of Nations, while her parents began consulting medical experts. From Hindi, English and India, Indira was now thrown into a background of French, German and Europe. Her privileged background notwithstanding, she soon took to life there so well that her self-reliance surprised everyone. As her father couldn't always accompany her, the eight year old soon became adept at changing buses and trams to school and back on her own as easily as any of the locals. Even the extreme cold and the snow that she encountered for the first time in her young life did not deter her. She revelled in snow fights with her Papu and squealed with delight when her snowballs found their mark.

Indira was happy. She had her parents to herself and saw them every day. They were finally a family. But she soon caught a chill and fell ill. Her worried parents thus pulled her out of L'Ecole and sent her to Chesieres, a family run boarding school in the Swiss mountains. They hoped the air there would do her good. It was not, however, a good choice as the staff members were all bullies and almost every student there was unhappy. Although Indira made some good friends, she didn't like Chesieres at all, though she did become an expert at skiing and skating. So despite having come to love the mountains as she did, her father took her out of school once again and sent her now to L'Ecole Nouvelle at Bex. It was closer to the sanatorium at Montana in the Alps where Kamala was being treated.

Indira thrived at Bex. Home during the weekends, she could ski to her heart's content with her father and visit with her mother constantly. And while her parents travelled whenever her mother was well, she was also sent on her own to a summer camp near Paris. But when they visited Germany and England, she too went with them. Soon, with her mother feeling much better though by no means fully recovered, they finally decided to return home. For Indira it meant new adjustments once again. But now a self-contained ten year old, she was a veteran having gone through six schools already.

Back in Allahabad she enrolled in St Mary's Convent run by German and British nuns. Indira, true to family tradition, was already a nationalist to the core. So once during Holi when one of the sisters took Indira and her classmates to task for playing with colours in school, Indira stood her ground. 'But it's Holi,' she said indignantly. 'So what? Don't talk back,' snapped the nun and punished her by ordering her to stand on the bench. They may have been strict and unused to Indian festivals, but the sisters also allowed Indira to take time off when necessary. So whenever her family decided to travel or when politics intervened or her mother fell ill, Indira missed school. Exams thus became of little consequence and organized education once again began to take a back seat. Politics soon began to creep back into her life as before.

Before long, following another miscarriage, Kamala fell ill once again. Twelve-year-old Indira was home tending her when Jawaharlal at the December 1929 Lahore session took over the Presidency of the Indian National Congress from his father. The entire family including Indira, was there camping out in the cold in tents to cheer him on. And when 'Purna Swaraj' meaning 'complete independence' was declared, the first person in the country to take the pledge was Indira herself. 'Read it out aloud,' her father told her. When she did so, he added, 'You are now committed to it.'

Back home at Anand Bhawan, on 26 January 1930 Indira, the youngest in the family, hoisted the flag of independence. The Congress tricolour with a charkha in the centre fluttered merrily in the breeze as she proudly recited the pledge and sang the anthem. (The Ashoka Chakra was to replace the charkha in the National Flag when India became independent in 1947). And on the same day, 26th of January twenty years later in 1950—celebrated as Republic Day ever since—India was to adopt a new constitution and become a Republic. Thus after a short lull Indira was once again in the thick of Indian politics. And she was not quite thirteen.

Soon after the declaration of Purna Swaraj the civil disobedience movement reached a new high and Jawaharlal Nehru became an iconic figure across the country. He was now 'Bharat Ratna' to the masses. A giggling Indira teased her Papu mercilessly when he was referred to as 'Thyagamurti' or idol of sacrifice.

A few months later in the March of 1930 Gandhiji

began a protest against a tax levied on salt. He led thousands of people into the sea to make their own salt in what has now become famous as the Dandi march. So first, her father and then her grandfather too were locked up along with Gandhiji. This time the Nehru men were imprisoned in Allahabad itself. Motilal Nehru fell seriously ill there. So he was released and allowed to go to Calcutta for treatment.

But soon the police swooped down on Anand Bhawan again. This time they came looking for Kamala. She was being arrested for her part in the protests. At dawn on New Year's Day (1931) Indira stood forlorn on the steps of Anand Bhawan watching her mother being taken way. Except for the servants, she was home alone again. Politics as usual was playing mayhem with her life.

Purna Swaraj

Lined by cheering and flag-waving crowds, the family watched with pride as Jawaharlal rode a white horse through the streets of Lahore to chair the opening sitting of the 1929 December session. By the time the session ended 'Purna Swaraj' had been declared. Its pledge ran thus:

> We believe that it is the inalienable right of the Indian people, as of any other people, to have freedom and to enjoy the fruits of their toil and have the necessities of life, so that they may have full opportunities of growth . . . We believe also that if

any government deprives a people of these rights and oppresses them, the people have a further right to alter it or to abolish it. The British government in India has not only deprived the Indian people of their freedom but has based itself on the exploitation of the masses, and has ruined India economically, politically, culturally, and spiritually. We believe, therefore, that India must sever the British connection and attain Purna Swaraj, or complete independence . . .

It would take another eighteen years of civil disobedience and non-violent protests before India would indeed win complete independence. But a formal beginning had been made.

7   Another World

It was now early February in 1931 and very cold in Allahabad. Anand Bhawan was spilling over with grieving people. In all the confusion no one appeared to notice her. A tall, thin girl with tears rolling down her cheeks, Indira stood aloof and alone in anguished silence. Her grandfather's body had just been brought home. Motilal Nehru had died in a Lucknow hospital shortly after he had returned from Calcutta following Kamala's arrest.

Grandparents are special, aren't they? And to lose them is always a tremendous shock especially if one was as warm and loving as Motilal was to Indira. She felt completely bereft. Her father—released from prison on compassionate grounds—and grandmother had been with him in his last moments. As she followed the cortège to the banks of the River Ganges where he was being cremated, it was evident to Indira that life for her would never be the same again.

She was not wrong. With Dadu gone and her parents completely involved in politics no one knew what to do with her. Since she could no longer be left unsupervised at home, they decided she should be sent to a residential school. This time it was Gandhiji who chose the school and he recommended one run by his good friends Mr and Mrs Vakil. But sadly it was in Poona, as far away from Allahabad as could be. So after a short holiday trip with her parents to Sri Lanka and parts of South India—to get over their grief—Indira joined Poona's Pupils' Own School. It was quite unlike any other school. Not only was it very spartan, it was informal and unconventional too. It also laid great emphasis on social work and national pride. She was there for three years—the longest she had ever spent at any school. Though Indira got on well with the Vakils, those three years were not exactly kind to her. Her mother, unwell again, was in hospital in Bombay while her father was in prison as usual. Her grandmother, now a frail old lady, was also injured, lathi charged and left to bleed on the streets while leading a peaceful demonstration.

The family came laden with sweets and chocolates as often as they could, but any news of her mother or father was generally only through letters or from the newspapers. She was often so lonely that other students would see her crying. Reserved and introverted as she was, she was too shy and proud to share her misery. Yet despite her unhappiness Indira took part in all school activities. She spent many hours trekking up the Western Ghats or organizing plays and raising funds for various social causes. When Gandhiji was imprisoned in the Yerawada jail in Poona, she became a regular visitor there and even went on sympathetic fasts with him. Her aunt Vijayalakshmi's children were sent to join her in school and a kind Indira often played mother to her three little homesick cousins.

It was 1934 and Indira's life was once again in limbo. She was sixteen and had passed her matriculation. Her stay at the Poona school was over. What next was the question. Tall, frail and still quite gawky, the tomboy was slowly turning into an appealingly attractive girl. But the struggle for independence going on in the background was still continuing to play havoc with her life. Her father was serving another two-year sentence in a Calcutta jail while her mother, extremely unwell again, was in a hospital near him. Her grandmother wanted her married off. But luckily for Indira, Kamala stood firm against this idea and so Indira was sent to Rabindranath Tagore's, Santiniketan near Calcutta. It was to later become the Visva-Bharati University. Her father, well aware of the upheavals in her life, wrote to Tagore: 'From her earliest childhood Indira has had to put up with national political troubles and domestic upheavals caused by them. Her education has suffered because of this and there has been no continuity in it. For long periods there has been no peace or quiet in her home atmosphere owing to her parent's and other relative's preoccupation with public affairs and often because of their absence in prison . . .' (*Indira Gandhi* by Zareer Masani)

So far removed was Santiniketan from anything she had been used to, it seemed to her like another world. There were no crowds, no political parleying nor any kind of upheavals. For the first time in her life she was her own mistress.

It was a beautiful campus, peaceful and quiet. With flowering bushes and many large trees it was like an ashram and Indira loved it. Yet life for the students was tough and demanding. The day began at 4 a.m. and they were expected to do their own cleaning, cooking and sweeping before class. There was no electricity or any of the normal necessities she was used to. She also had to share a room with three other girls. Lessons started at six in the morning and were held under trees. Apprehensive though she had been at first, Indira took to life at Santiniketan without a problem.

Her father wrote to her often and sent her books. And Santiniketan introduced her to a world of art, music and dance for the first time. So although her father kept urging her to do well in academics, she told him, 'I find my fine art classes far more interesting, Papu.' And she did so well in classical Indian dance, especially Manipuri, that she was soon taking part in school performances. Initially in awe of him, she also soon began to enjoy her interactions with Rabindranath Tagore.

Indira continued to be reserved and introverted but in Santiniketan, far away from the chaotic world of politics, she actually blossomed. Her fun-loving nature was often belied by her shy and serious manner and many unsuspecting lecturers fell victim to her pranks. 'Shall we stage a silent walk out to teach ill-mannered Mr Fabri (the art history teacher) a lesson?' she asked her classmates mischievously one day. And they did exactly that. On another occasion, to the glee of her classmates, she hid the batik bag of a boastful teacher from right under her nose. But as much as she loved her new environment and looked up to her new mentor Rabindranath Tagore,

Indira missed her mother dreadfully and was constantly anxious about her health. Sadly, Kamala's condition worsened all of a sudden and once again Indira's rather chequered education took another turn.

Rabindranath Tagore

Rabindranath Tagore, otherwise known as Gurudev, was one of India's greatest poets. He was also a playwright, composer and author. He founded the Visva-Bharati University at Santiniketan near Calcutta, combining western and Indian methods of teaching. In 1913 Rabindranath Tagore won the Nobel Prize for his book of poems *Gitanjali* after he happened to translate them from Bengali to English. *Gitanjali* became an instant hit. In 1915 he was knighted by King George V of England but when the Jallianwala Bagh massacre occurred, Tagore renounced his knighthood in protest.

Tagore wrote about a thousand poems, eight books of short stories, two dozen plays and eight novels apart from various books on educational and social subjects. He also has to his credit two thousand songs known as Rabindra Sangeet. Two of them are the national anthems of India and Bangladesh today. His paintings too can be found in various museums. He was a creative genius and one of India's literary greats.

Mummie's Best Friend

'Do you know anything about what happens at home when you are absent?' wrote Indira from Santiniketan to her father imprisoned in Dehradun. 'Do you know that when Mummy was in a very bad condition the house was full of people but not one of them even went to see her or sit awhile with her, that when she was in agony there was no one to help her?' (*Indira* by Katherine Frank).

Kamala was gravely ill with pleurisy. Pleurisy is a disease that attacks the lungs by filling it up with fluid. It could turn fatal if not treated in time. And a weak Kamala already ravaged by TB was not only running a high temperature, she was also finding it hard to breathe.

So Indira had been summoned from Santiniketan and Jawaharlal was released from jail on compassionate grounds. But when her condition improved slightly and her fever came down, Jawaharlal had to go back to prison while Indira returned to Santiniketan. Indira was now not just worried and anxious, she was angry and upset too. On rushing home she had found her mother lying unattended and neglected in her room. Indira noticed that except for Kamala's doctor cousin, Madan Bhai, everybody else began to gather around Kamala and display concern only when her father arrived. She feared that with her father gone and she in Santiniketan nobody would bother to take care of Kamala properly.

This was not the first time that she had come to her mother's defence. Indira, even as a little girl, realized that her shy mother was rather out of her depth in the Nehru household. Kamala, though hailing from a wealthy and aristocratic background, had come into a westernized household that was totally different from what she had been used to. She was a simple person, unschooled in western ways and not as sophisticated as the Nehru girls. Their superior attitude towards her was made worse by her own persistent poor health.

Vijayalakshmi, the older of Jawaharlal's two sisters, was only a year younger than Kamala and she perhaps was not very nice to her. But Motilal Nehru was very fond of his daughter-in-law. Why, hadn't he himself personally chosen her as a bride for his adored son? Her domineering mother-in-law, Swaroop Rani, saw Kamala as a sweet but high-spirited girl who could be managed while Krishna, the younger sister loved and admired her.

Vijayalakshmi adored her brother and was quite possessive of him so it's quite possible that there was a bit of sibling jealousy at play here. So she apparently made life miserable not only for Kamala but for Indira as well. As for Jawaharlal, who was quite the westernized ladies' man, he initially found Kamala's shyness and lack of sophistication quite daunting. But before long, her genuineness and sincerity won him over. However, he does regret in later life that because he was caught up in India's struggle for independence, he was guilty of not spending as much time with her as he should have. Nevertheless despite her husband's lack of attention and her own frequent bouts of ill health, Kamala managed to carve out a life for herself.

She had her own views of the independence struggle and got on well with Gandhiji. She actively supported her husband and encouraged him when his father was against Jawaharlal joining the civil disobedience movement. When not unwell she worked side by side with Congress volunteers and encouraged women across the country to heed Gandhiji's call to step out of their homes and join their men in the struggle for independence. At heart a true feminist, she implored women to drop their purdahs and fight for their freedom. And when she too was arrested she went happily to their 'other home' regardless of how it would affect her ailing health. But for her illness Kamala would have easily become a champion of women's causes.

In fact her participation in politics won her the admiration of the people and Jawaharlal belatedly began to appreciate his wife's many sterling qualities. And when the time came she even stood in for her husband at political meetings and hartals. It was on one such occasion that a Congress worker called Feroze Gandhi came into their lives. He was the son of a Parsi shopkeeper and was not, despite the common surname, related to Gandhiji. Once while out picketing, Kamala had been in danger of being lathi charged. Feroze jumped in to save her and ever since remained a devoted friend. But all that was to come later.

For the better part of her short life Kamala had to at home put up with subtle and not so subtle insults about her lack of sophistication and non-western background. Indira, who noticed all this, was upset. She tried hard to convince her father and grandfather about what was going on. But they were indifferent and uninterested. Indira loved her beautiful mother deeply. She also felt somehow responsible for her. Though a mere child she resented their unkindness fiercely. She often argued and quarrelled with people if she thought her mother was being mistreated. Thus with every rebuke and reprimand that came Kamala's way, Indira's role as her mother's defender became more and more pronounced.

Indira may have been her loyal knight but Kamala too was her daughter's main support and the person who kept her grounded. She had her own ideas of how she wanted her daughter to be. It was she who encouraged Indira to stand on her own feet and be independent. And when Kamala found that her jewellery too was disappearing the same way as her father-in-law's wealth, she quickly created a financial trust to secure her daughter's future.

Kamala was spiritual too. She taught Indira Hindi and introduced her to Hindu scriptures. She encouraged Jawaharlal and Indira to read the Bhagvad Gita with her every morning. Her father believed he was the one who moulded his daughter's thinking, but Indira always felt that it was her mother's strong sense of values that she had absorbed. However, more than anything else it was her mother's humiliation in her own household that profoundly impacted and influenced Indira. 'I saw her being hurt and I was determined not to be hurt,' she was to say later (*Mother India* by Pranay Gupte).

Since, latest bout of pleurisy had left Kamala gravely ill, she was soon shifted to the Bhowali sanatorium near Almora in the Himalayas. Indira feared her mother's condition was worsening. She was not wrong. The doctors soon decided Kamala needed to go to Europe for further treatment.

The Nehru Sisters

In north India when girls get married it is often customary to give them new names when they go to their husband's homes. So Sarup who was also called 'Nan' became Vijayalakshmi, when she married Ranjit Pandit, a brilliant lawyer. Her wedding was a magnificent affair and was one of the last grand occasions celebrated at Anand Bhawan. She got married in a pink saree woven in fine khadi by Gandhiji's wife Kasturba.

Vijayalakshmi took part in the freedom movement and was jailed twice, at first in 1932 and then during the Quit India Movement in 1942. Like her sister Krishna, Vijayalakhmi did not have any formal schooling. Yet she rose to become the president of the UN General Assembly and free India's ambassador to several countries. She was elected to Parliament from Phulpur, her brother's constituency. She has also published a few books. But she never got over her dislike of her niece and when Indira became prime minister in 1966, she retired from politics. Vijayalakhsmi finally settled in Dehradun where she died in 1990. She had three daughters.

Krishna, also known as Betty, loved Kamala and adored Indira. Indira herself looked up to her 'chitti' (aunt, in Tamil) and always turned to her whenever she needed help. Krishna's wedding to Raja Hutheesingh was a rather quiet affair unlike her sister's. Krishna too was a published author. She had two sons. She died while she was abroad but she lived to see Indira become prime minister. She says of her niece 'I have loved her too much to find any shortcomings in Indira . . . she is a true daughter of our family.'

9   A Changing World

The sudden storm surprised Indira. The thunder sounded alarmingly loud and the eerie flashes of lightening among the trees were scary. The mist too seemed to suddenly envelope her. The Black Forests are known for their sudden fiery storms and a terrified Indira would often be caught in them. For barely a year after she joined Santiniketan, Indira was out and on the move again. Her father, who was still in prison, had sent for her. He told her to accompany her mother and Madan Bhai to Europe because he could not make the journey himself. Suddenly Indira was all packed and gone from Santiniketan, never to return. She had admired Gurudev deeply, and unconventional though it had been, loved being part of university life. But naturally her mother's health came first. Tagore too was sorry to see her go.

Now from Bhowali, in Uttarakhand, it was to a remote sanatorium in Badenweiler in the Black Forests of Bavaria in Germany that the seventeen-year-old Indira accompanied her ailing mother. She could only visit Kamala twice a day so she stayed in a guest house nearby. Thus alone in her room, apart from the anxiety over her mother the lonely adolescent had to contend with the fury of these frightening storms as well.

Now hurrying to get out of it she could feel the intense cold of the rain. Shadows too seemed to be popping up from nowhere. It brought back memories of the terror she used to feel as a child when she was made to walk to her room at night in Allahabad.

Indira remembered how petrified she had been of lurking shadows. Anand Bhawan was so large and dark they seemed to be everywhere. Her parents would insist she walk to her room alone after dinner every night. It was their idea of developing her courage. But how she wished she didn't have to. Along the garden, through the long veranda with its dimly lit staircases, her imagination working overtime, she would visualize terrifying monsters waiting to pounce on her from behind the pillars. Even if she had complained, her father would have only told her not to act spoilt. Now far away from home and with a sick mother, she had no other option. She had to fend for herself. Like always.

But soon, to Indira's delight, Kamala seemed to be regaining her health. Especially after Jawaharlal was released from jail and allowed to join them. Life turned bright for a brief while and Indira and her father spent many companionable hours by her mother's bedside. Indira also went for long walks exploring the countryside. Sadly a few months later Kamala moved hospitals again. This time to a sanatorium in Lausanne and Indira, now back at her old school in Bex, knew her mother was dangerously ill once again.

In the midst of all their anxiety there was one person who came to see them often. Feroze Gandhi. He was

Kamala's young Congress-worker friend from Allahabad who had been constantly in and out of their lives in the past. He had many a time selflessly nursed Kamala—last in Bhowali—whenever Jawaharlal was in prison. Feroze was studying at the London School of Economics and frequently came over to keep them company. And he was by their side when within a month of moving to Lausanne, Kamala, who had just turned thirty-six, finally gave up on life. Even the night before, Indira had sat with her mother well past midnight. Kamala had not only been her daughter's main support but also her husband's silent strength. A heartbroken Indira stood sadly by her grieving father as her mother was cremated in an alien country far away from home.

Jawaharlal now felt that Indira should remain behind and prepare for Oxford while he returned to India. She obeyed. But feeling lost and vulnerable without her mother, she soon moved to London. Luckily Feroze, who was already living there, was at hand to look after her and introduce her around. She met with many renowned intellectuals and world leaders who were all delighted to see the famous Jawaharlal Nehru's daughter. Having been away for so long and fretting for home, Indira was no longer interested in academics. She was keener on what was happening politically in India and around her. So she dabbled in India League activities and debated British politics instead of concentrating on her studies. And to her father's disappointment failed to find a place in Oxford.

Always prone to chills, Indira now unexpectedly fell very ill. She went home. But it was a brief visit. Even so, having turned twenty-one she grabbed the opportunity to finally become a member of the Congress Party. With her tonsils out, however, she was soon deemed fit and sent back to the exclusive Badminton School in Bristol to prepare again for Oxford. This time she was successful. She got into Somerville College and read modern history till 1939 when she again caught a bad chill. With memories of her mother's illness fresh in their minds, Indira was sent swiftly to convalesce in Switzerland. She was away for almost eleven months.

Indira now totally lost all interest in her studies and wasn't keen on going back to Oxford. Especially as she had failed some of her papers. She was also worried about her father. Her grandmother had died, her two aunts were married and her father was alone. So she told him, 'Papu I am coming home for good. I have been away for five years and I miss home.' Though he had been the one who had earlier insisted she stay back, Jawaharlal was quietly relieved. He was in fact very lonely and longing to have her back. In any case with Europe right in the middle of another world war it was not the right time to be in England.

Regular commercial flights were still a few years away and so people usually travelled between continents on ocean liners. It took about a month by sea to reach India from England. And so in 1941 to avoid the ongoing war Indira set sail for India via Durban. She was returning home with Feroze. They were in love. He had constantly been by her side these past few years. Six years to the day she had sailed out with Kamala as an unsure and insecure young girl, Indira was going back to India, a more poised and self-reliant young lady but without her mother and without a degree.

Second World War

The Second World War started in 1939 and ended in 1945. After the First World War defeat Germany felt humiliated. She was waiting for a chance to regain the territories she had lost and she got her opportunity under Adolf Hitler. Hitler began to expand and invade other European countries one by one. He formed an alliance with Japan and Italy who wanted to expand their own borders as well. When Hitler after swallowing practically half of Europe finally marched into Poland, Britain in self-defence entered the war. Australia, New Zealand, Canada, South Africa soon joined her and they became the 'allies' along with the USSR. Now as the allies took on the axis powers the war stretched across continents. When Japan attacked the US by bombing Pearl Harbour, America too joined the allies and dropped an atom bomb on the Japanese towns of Hiroshima and Nagasaki annihilating millions. Japan surrendered. The Polish and Soviet troops too now fought back and captured Germany's capital Berlin and the allies defeated the axis troops in North Africa and Italy as well. And when Hitler committed suicide it effectively ended the Second World War. The United Nations was formed to prevent further conflicts and the world was reorganized into two blocs with the USA and USSR emerging as two superpowers.

10   Her Dadu and Her Papu

Indira had been devastated by her mother's death. She had felt the same way when her beloved grandfather 'Dadu' had passed away five years ago. Her grandfather at that point of time had been the most important person in her life. She had admired his larger-than-life personality and as she was to say later, 'I loved the way he laughed . . . And when he laughed the whole house sort of shook and laughed with him.'(*Indira Gandhi* by Pupul Jayakar). Hanging around him constantly, she had continuously pestered him with questions. Questions he always answered patiently, however frivolous. Nothing had been too small or unimportant where his 'Indu' was concerned. He had in fact doted on her. Her aunt Krishna says Motilal Nehru, who was usually quick to temper and very strict with his own children, was completely the opposite with his little granddaughter. He was very proud of her and often showed her off to visitors.

As a little girl tearing around the house in high spirits, she often barged into her grandfather's study yelling, 'No admission without permission.' She knew he was busy and she shouldn't be disturbing him but she also knew she would get away with it. Though her parents often did, her Dadu never reprimanded her.

A brilliant lawyer, Motilal was also an anglophile, who admired English culture and life. So in a western-styled house he lived the life of an aristocratic Englishman in India and brought up his three children in the same disciplined British manner—with governesses and regular holidays in Mussoorie and other hill stations. They were also encouraged to always speak, read and write in English. But when it came to Indira, all discipline and routine, British or otherwise, went out through the window. Primarily because by then, he was completely caught up in the freedom struggle.

Thus whenever Motilal Nehru was home, Anand Bhawan became a beehive of activity. As he had wholeheartedly begun to support the idea of a free India, consultations and arguments also became a part of everyone's life. With people like Gandhiji and Muhammad Ali Jinnah constantly visiting, excitement ran high when strategies and theories on how to handle the British were debated and worked upon.

Indira, pitchforked into this political world that her folks inhabited, listened and absorbed as unobtrusively as she could. In fact the discussions and political meetings happening around her may have subconsciously moulded and shaped her own future political identity. Gandhiji, who was extremely fond of her, impressed her with his political wisdom and as for her father, she hero-worshipped him. Nevertheless, it was her Dadu who wielded tremendous influence over her during her early years. Much more in fact than her Papu. Even so her father was soon to become a more dominant force in her life.

Schooled at one of Britain's premier public schools, Harrow, and holding a Tripos from the University of Cambridge, Jawaharlal was also a barrister. But Gandhiji's call for a non-violent rebellion against the British so galvanized him that he was soon completely involved in the freedom struggle. If he was not out picketing or chalking out strategies, he was being thrown into jail. Otherwise he was traversing the dusty villages of India learning how to reach out to the people. Hence he had little or almost no time for his young family. Realizing that his daughter was more or less growing up without him, he sought to remain a part of her life. He tried to do that through letters.

In the summer of 1928 when she was about eleven years old, he started to write to her. 'When you and I are together, you often ask me questions about many things and I try to answer them. Now that you are in Mussoorie and I am in Allahabad we cannot have these talks. I am therefore going to write to you from time to time short accounts of the story of our earth and the many countries, great and small, into which it is divided . . .' (*Letters from a Father to his Daughter* by Jawaharlal Nehru).

He initially wrote about thirty letters to her telling her about the world of nature, how early history was written and how the earth was formed. Reminding her of all the interesting things they had seen in museums abroad, he spoke about the first living things, animals and the coming of man and different races. He then told her how religion even though it first evolved out of fear—which was bad since anything done out of fear is not good—actually told them many beautiful things. He described different civilizations and cultures, including China and Egypt, and concluded it with the epics and the arrival of the Aryans in India.

He was in fact trying to introduce her to a world other than politics. By and large, these series of letters made up for the lack of organized education in Indira's life. Indira enjoyed her father's correspondence. It opened up for her a whole new world. But more than that it told her that he truly loved and missed her. Later published as a book trated *Letters from a Father to His Daughter*, these letters are today as relevant and fascinating as they were eighty-five years ago.

A few years later in the October of 1930, Jawaharlal began another series of letters to Indira from the central jail in Naini. 'For Indira Priyadarshini on her thirteenth birthday' it said and dealt now with the history of the world from ancient times. It comprised a hundred and ninety-six letters in the form of chapters. Called *Glimpses of World History* it remains, as Indira herself said, 'The best introduction to the story of man for young and growing people and indeed all over the world.'

All in all till she turned fifteen, Indira must have received more than two hundred letters from her father. They were actually what kept her in touch with him during her entire childhood. They brought him closer to her and also broadened her horizons. He also sent her books regularly and told her what to read. She became a voracious reader who not only enjoyed plays and poetry but also read serious biographies and treatises far in advance of her years.

But Jawaharlal was also at times quite thoughtless and negligent of her feelings. When Indira was leaving Bhowali for Europe with her ailing mother she was surprised to receive a letter from her father summarily informing her he was handing over their house—Anand Bhawan—to her aunt Vijaylakshmi. 'Your room is to be given to them. Kamala's and my rooms are to remain unchanged so if you want to put any of your personal effects apart, you may put them in my room but I do not want my room to be converted into a luggage room.' (*Indira Gandhi* by Pupul Jayakar)

How do you think that made poor Indira feel? Her room to be given away to an aunt who was certainly not her favourite person? It probably never struck Jawaharlal that she might feel upset or that he was depriving her of her only home. Indira did as he ordered and though Anand Bhawan was eventually left to her in his will, she was deeply hurt. She took her revenge years later when she denied her aunt permission to stay there even for a night—yes, Indira could be vindictive too!

Jawaharlal also often discussed matters of the state with his daughter. He took her on trips to Southeast Asian countries like Malaysia, Burma and Singapore and introduced her to other cultures. And in between her Oxford stint they also visited France, Czechoslovakia and

Hungary. So by the time she was twenty-four and sailing home for good, Indira had already been exposed to a mixture of other international cultures and politics. She knew more about world affairs than most girls her age.

Muhammad Ali Jinnah

Muhammad Ali Jinnah, considered the founder of Pakistan, was its first Governor General. He was born into a Gujarati family in Karachi, lived in Bombay and practised law. Demanding that the rights of the Muslims in British India be protected, he put forth the Two Nation Theory. The British agreed to partition India and Pakistan was created. Jinnah died a year later after laying the foundation of the new nation. He was married to a Parsi—Rutan-Bai Petit and had one daughter, Dina. The house he built—Jinnah House—still exists on Malabar Hill, Bombay.

11   Politics in Her Blood

Indira was happy to be going home. She felt lost without her mother and she missed her father. She also missed being part of the political scene in India.

She had been a toddler in her mother's arms when politics had first entered their home. Her grandfather had given her a charkha to spin her own khadi when she was just five. And she had got the Bal Charkha Sangh in Allahabad up and running for Gandhiji by the time she was seven. Her life had thus, even as a child, swung like a pendulum to the beat of Indian nationalism. Now she longed to be part of it all over again.

Standing on the deck of the ship with the breeze in her face she remembered how as a child despite being lonely and insecure she had never lacked in patriotic fervour or imagination.

She recollected how she had cleverly devised her own games. Dressing her dolls up in kurta pajamas and making them carry flags like Congress volunteers, she had lined them up against tin policemen who carried lathis. Then, if not pitting them against each other, she would collect the servants around her and exhort them in the same manner as she had heard her father or Gandhiji, to be brave and to rebel against the British.

One day her aunt had found her on the balcony railing with her arm outstretched. Eyes closed she was waving it around as if she was fencing. 'What in the world are you doing?' Krishna asked. 'I am practising to be Joan of Arc. One day like her I will lead my people to freedom,' replied Indira without breaking stride. Joan of Arc was a French heroine who is famous for having fought the British bravely. She was finally burnt at the stake but not before she had won many battles. So in the politically charged environment of the time, Indira had even as a child already begun to see herself as a 'Joan'—a protector of her country and her people.

Thinking back, Indira realized that politics had even dictated what she wore. She had been a thin, spindly girl with short hair and like the Congress volunteers always dressed in kurta pajamas with a topi on her head. And she had loved to confuse strangers. Pretending to be a boy she would first welcome guests in her kurta pajama then quickly change into a frock and go in to greet them again. Only to be asked where her brother was—which naturally caused a lot of amusement all round! So often was she mistaken for a boy that she even took to calling herself 'Indu boy'.

Every Sunday she would enthusiastically cycle six miles to the house of Sam Higginbotham, an American missionary, to help his wife sort out donations of clothes, toys and books for children at a leper home. 'How many other seven year olds would do that when they could be out playing?' Indira now wondered. The idea of helping others less fortunate had obviously already caught her imagination because everyone around her was doing just that.

Indira had also been among the first to help when a section of Anand Bhawan had been converted into a hospital to nurse injured activists. A seriously wounded young boy who lived to tell the tale recalled twenty years later how devotedly the little girl had nursed him. Thanks to her family, so caught up was she in the politics of the country it is doubtful whether she saw herself as anything other than a Congress volunteer in the service of her nation.

She also clearly remembered the day when as a twelve year old she had walked up to the Congress Party office and asked to be made a member. Her request had been flatly turned down. 'Come back when you are older,' they told her. Angry, she had decided then and there that she needed to do something about it. With her mother's help she collected all the children around her and organized her own little band of troops. She called it Vanar Sena after Hanuman's famous monkey army that helped Rama conquer Lanka in the epic Ramayana. Her grandfather and the other members of her family were greatly amused. But this little army with Indira as its general came in very useful to the activists. They ran errands, pasted bills, wrote notices, made flags, smuggled messages and spied on police stations.

Indira even managed to fool the police a few times and to smuggle out secret documents for her father. Like the time when a suspicious policeman stopped her car with the plans of the civil disobedience movement hidden in the boot. She knew if found, it would spell danger for her father and his associates. Her heart in her mouth Indira calmly pleaded with him. 'Please don't search the car now. I'm already very late for school.' The policeman believed Indira and let her go.

She had been politically quite savvy too. When Gandhiji decided to participate in the Round Table Conference of 1931, she apparently quite boldly told him that had her grandfather been alive, he wouldn't have allowed him to come to terms with the British.

She also now recalled in embarrassment her latest fiasco. Indira was at Oxford when she was deputed to read out a message on behalf of her father at an India League meeting in London. She landed up there only to find to her dismay that she was required to make a speech. When she attempted to do so, somebody in the room remarked that 'she doesn't speak, she squeaks'. While the room burst into laughter, it sent Indira to tears and brought her oration to an abrupt end. She swore she would never speak publicly again. However, she was to soon find out that speeches were not too difficult when one believed in something passionately.

The ship soon docked at Durban, South Africa. The excited Indian community came aboard to welcome the legendary Nehru's daughter and take her around to show her the sights. Indira was shocked and appalled to see the pathetic condition of the Africans in their ghettos. And at a reception organized for her, Indira, who had earlier told her hosts she wouldn't take the stage because she was not good at public speaking, involuntarily rose to her feet and burst into a passionate speech, 'How can they be treated so shabbily?' she asked. 'Why are you Indians aligning yourselves with these whites and not helping the black people?' Her speech upset her hosts and surprised herself as well. Evidently if worked up or angry she could deliver hard-hitting speeches anytime, anywhere.

Raised as she was and bred into it, politics quite evidently ran in her very blood. Was it any wonder that she was eager to reach home? Especially as the Indian National Congress was refusing to participate in the Second World War and Gandhiji had started a no-war Satyagraha?

Indira and Bapu

Apart from her grandfather and her father, the one other person who influenced Indira's life hugely was Gandhiji. She was only two years old when he first came to Anand Bhawan and she was not quite five when she went visiting Bapu at his Sabarmati Ashram. Since then, playing the role of a loving uncle Gandhiji took an interest in whatever she did. He not only played mediator when her father and grandfather differed on how and where she was to be educated, he also encouraged her to take part in the freedom struggle, wrote to her often and even tried to allay her fears when she was low and unhappy. He supported her when she wanted to marry Feroze and persuaded her father to agree to the match.

He even wrote an open letter in a newspaper to placate the country when it objected to her marriage. On her part Indira may not have always agreed with Gandhiji but she always looked up to him as an elder of the family, discussed her problems with him, visited him in jail whenever she could and even went on token fasts with him. Just the day before he was assassinated, Indira had taken her little son Rajiv to visit him. Rajiv had gathered some flowers and put them at Gandhiji's feet.

12   Family Ties

Indira was about thirteen when she happened to overhear one of her aunts refer to her as an 'ugly and stupid child'. (*Indira Gandhi* by Pupul Jayakar) Could her aunt be right she wondered? Was she really ugly and stupid? Did everyone else think the same, she asked herself?

And the damage was done. As Indira herself says, 'It blighted my entire youth.' Indira was deeply wounded. She was a sensitive girl and since no one refuted the remark, she believed it. Her confidence plunged and she began to lose self-esteem. If only she had discussed this with her mother or someone who cared for her they would have told her it wasn't true. But since she didn't, Indira began to see herself the way her aunt described her, which was sad, as it was evident her aunt—probably because Indira always defended Kamala—did not like her and so her judgement was bound to be coloured by her dislike. But as an adolescent, Indira was too young to realize that such remarks were not necessarily true.

Notwithstanding her insecure and lonely childhood she had been a lively little girl. But now in her teens she became reserved and withdrawn. If upset, she often retreated into a cold silence. And as she grew into a young lady, unable to forget those remarks, she became wary of trusting people. She was perhaps comfortable only with people like her mother's young friend Feroze, for instance, who had known her for years, ever since her teens.

Now on her way home from England with him she realized that she could think of no better person than Feroze as her husband. They had been together these last few years and he had become a good companion and friend. He had been there for her when her mother died and even after. Just five years older, he was a brash, sunny natured man full of good humour. 'Marry me please,' he had begged her often even when Kamala had been alive.

But as they belonged to different communities both families were against the marriage. He was a Parsi and she a Hindu and as her father told her, their backgrounds were also totally different. Jawaharlal believed she would not be happy with Feroze. She was also from one of India's most aristocratic families while Feroze was not. The nation too disapproved of Indira Nehru entering into an inter-caste wedding. It caused a furore across the country. But Indira couldn't care less. She was adamant. 'I will marry him,' she said. So Gandhiji stepped in. He persuaded her father to give in. He also managed to pacify an agitated country.

On 26 March 1942, almost a year and a half after they returned home, a lovely Indira in a simple pink khadi saree studded with tiny silver stars—spun by her father in jail—became Mrs Feroze Gandhi. The wedding was an elegant 'vedic' affair. Crowds of party workers and volunteers were in attendance and every treetop in and around Anand Bhawan had people straining to catch a glimpse of the bride. She wore no jewellery except for some flowers, an armlet and glass bangles. Yet she looked beautiful. But her eyes which occasionally glanced at the vacant cushion by her father's side spoke of a hidden sadness. She must have missed her mother's presence. Indira's wedding too, like her life so far, was played out in the backdrop of hectic political activity. The Cripps Mission from Britain was in India for talks, and discussions to chalk out the Congress response were held in between the wedding ceremonies.

Soon after a happy honeymoon in Kashmir, Indira and Feroze returned to Allahabad. Not to Anand Bhawan but to a small rented two-room apartment. Almost immediately the couple plunged into political activity organizing rallies, marches and secret rendezvous for Congress activists.

In August 1942 Feroze, a seasoned Congressman— having been jailed four times already—with Indira attended the special two-day Bombay meeting of the Indian National Congress where Nehru as Congress President seconded Gandhiji's call and urged all Indians to renew their struggle to throw the British out of India. The British retaliated brutally. They fired upon the protesters and lathi charged them mercilessly. They also imprisoned all the major leaders. However, the Quit India Movement took on a mass momentum of its own and spread rapidly. Scores were killed and thousands injured.

Soon the police with guns and tear shells pounced on a defiant Indira addressing a public meeting. Feroze rushed to her aid. Both were jailed.

Feroze was locked up in the men's section of the Naini jail and Indira was sent to join her aunt Vijayalakshmi, who was already imprisoned in the women's section. With her cousin Chandralekha, Vijayalakshmi's daughter, who was also in jail with them, they were kept six to a cell. Now, Indira finally got to live in their 'other home'—a place where her family had spent so much of their lives. She also celebrated her twenty-fifth birthday there.

Indira was imprisoned for nine months and she says that only those who have gone to jail can know how one's spirit slowly turns numb and how each day seems as long as a year. But it was she who nevertheless made them all comfortable. She converted the cell into a cosy little playhouse where they could enact plays and hold reading sessions. The jail cat she mischievously named 'Mehitabel' after the alley cat in the then popular Don Marquis adventure stories of *Archy and Mehitabel*, the broken tap without a head was the 'Headless Earl' and one half of the cell laid out in a blue sheet from home became the 'Blue Drawing Room'. They kept diaries and Indira wrote hers in French! Her father in the meanwhile was confined in the Ahmednagar Fort.

As she soon fell quite ill, Indira had to be released. A few months later, so was Feroze. They now decided to move into Anand Bhawan. Her father was happy: the house would once more house the family. But Bengal was right then in the grip of a terrible famine, so Indira was soon out and about raising funds for the hungry and the needy.

On 20 August 1944 her eldest son Rajiv, named after Kamala (lotus), was born. Indira went to her aunt Krishna in Bombay to have her baby but it was to be almost a year before her imprisoned father would see his grandson for the first time. With the freedom struggle peaking, Delhi was where the action was. So Jawaharlal when released moved there to a small house on York Road while the young family moved from Allahabad to Lucknow where Feroze took charge of the *National Herald*, a newspaper founded by his father-in-law. They were a happy little family for a while.

Events were slowly propelling India towards independence and all the major leaders were involved in hectic political parleying. Indira, who had purposely stayed out of politics after Rajiv's birth, now began to shuttle between Lucknow and Delhi. Stressed out with work, her father needed her around. In 1946 on the 14th of December, her younger son Sanjay was born. Seven months later in 1947, on the 15th of August, his grandfather assumed leadership of an independent India. The entire nation erupted in joy and Indira's happiness was no less than any of the actual participants who had made it happen. Hadn't her entire life been dependent on the demands of these very same politics?

However, horrendous Hindu-Muslim riots broke out soon after the Partition and Indira, who was in Mussoorie with the children, was on her way back.

Looking out of the train window she saw a man being lynched by a mob. Unafraid she jumped out, stood between the hapless man and the crowd, and saved him. When she again fearlessly affected another similar rescue, Gandhiji, who had sent her out to work in the riot-torn areas, told her, 'Your education hasn't been in vain. I am proud of you.' The very next day Gandhiji himself was shot dead. It was 30 January 1948. A shocked nation in stunned disbelief heard Jawaharlal Nehru say, 'The light has gone out of our lives and there is darkness everywhere . . . our beloved leader, Bapu as we called him, the Father of the Nation, is no more . . .'

The same year Jawaharlal Nehru officially moved into what is now Teen Murti House as prime minister. His daughter and her family soon followed.

Jawaharlal Nehru's Address to the Nation
India attained her independence on 15 August 1947. At midnight on the 14th of August, celebrating crowds dancing with joy on the streets heard Jawaharlal Nehru proudly announce:

> Long years ago, we made a tryst with destiny. Now the time comes when we shall redeem our pledge, not wholly or in full measure, but very substantially. At the stroke of the midnight hour when the world sleeps, India will awake to life and

freedom. It is fitting that at this solemn moment, we take the pledge of dedication to the service of India and her people, and to the still larger cause of humanity . . . this is no time for petty and destructive criticism, no time for ill will or blaming others. We have to build the noble mansion of free India where all her children may dwell . . .

Jawaharlal Nehru was sworn in as independent India's first prime minister the next day. He was to serve for seventeen years.

13   Teen Murti House

Peals of laughter echoed across the house. Bhimsa the panda had escaped again. As he raced through the house with Indira chasing him, Rajiv and Sanjay could hardly contain their boyish mirth. Their grandfather Jawaharlal Nehru was expecting some important leaders for lunch and Indira was trying in vain to get their red Himalayan pet panda back into his den before they arrived.

In red and cream sandstone, Teen Murti House (it has three statues of soldiers outside its gates) was an enormous house with sprawling grounds. It had been the official residence of the Commander-in-Chief of the British-Indian Army and was now the residence of the new prime minister of independent India. And for a long time it was known simply as the prime minister's house before it became Teen Murti House. But to the boys it seemed more like a palace. Their grandfather had asked their mother to act as his official hostess and so their father Feroze himself had suggested they move to Delhi while he stayed back in Lucknow. He felt the constant shunting between Lucknow and Delhi was telling on Indira's fragile health.

Feroze had also promised to visit as often as he could. And he did, initially, quite frequently. All the same the boys missed being around him. Feroze was good with his hands and if he wasn't making toys he was assembling models of cars, planes and even trains for them. He was an outgoing man with a tremendous sense of fun. He loved the boys and was, in short, a good father.

Their mother too was no less a good parent. She was a 'hands-on' mom. Despite her now hectic schedule she saw to their every need and always made sure they were all right. In fact she was a super mom. She even won America's best 'Mothers' Award' once. How many mothers, they wondered, would keep awake half the night with a sick tiger cub? That's exactly what she did when one of their cubs had fallen ill. They had three now, plus a crocodile. They had actually a veritable zoo in their enormous backyard. Apart from Bhimsa and his mate, they had so many dogs, parrots, turtles and other forms of animal life that they were still counting.

The long corridors and the huge grounds which had seemed so formidable when they first moved in now appeared just right not only for their little animal farm but also for their games of cops and robbers and cowboys and Indians. They even had a snug little wigwam in a corner far away from the main house where their grandfather's guests would sometimes join them at play. All in all the prime minister's house was great fun. Sadly, studies beckoned and the boys had to soon leave for Dehradun to attend school. Though they had their holidays to look forward to.

Feroze's frequent visits to Delhi now began to dwindle especially as Indira grew into her role as her father's busy hostess. She had always disliked socializing and usually avoided parties. But now she soon became adept at both. Many of the world's top leaders came to stay with them and often told Nehru what a lovely hostess his daughter was. She also now began accompanying her father on his travels abroad—to China to meet the leader Chou Enlai, to the UK to attend the new queen's coronation and then twice to the USSR. Charmed with her elegance and grace many Russians of the time even named their babies 'Indira'. Jawaharlal soon began to consult his daughter and use her as a sounding board. She too began to form her own opinions just like she used to as a child in Anand Bhawan.

Feroze now decided he wanted to enter politics. He gave up his job with the *National Herald* in Lucknow and stood as a candidate in the country's first 1951–'52 general elections. Indira campaigned extensively for him, as did her father, and Feroze was elected handsomely from Rae Bareli. He was to win again from this constituency in 1957.

Now a Member of Parliament he joined his family in Teen Murti House. But when allotted a government house as an MP, he moved out as he found the protocol and code of behaviour in the prime minister's house quite restrictive. Feroze was an honest but opinionated man and his views often clashed with those of his father-in-law who was himself short-tempered. It was embarrassing for Indira, who always desperately tried to maintain peace.

Feroze was determined to expose the misdeeds of business houses and the corruption in the government. This brought him into conflict with those in power. Most of them were unfortunately people his father-in-law trusted implicitly. In fact Feroze was responsible for the act passed in 1956 that gave the press freedom to report on parliamentary proceedings. Though he and his father-in-law did not get on, Feroze was a popular man with a large circle of friends and admirers.

And then although they continued to be extremely fond of each other, as Indira herself began to take an active part in national politics, Feroze and Indira gradually began drifting apart as a couple. However, when Feroze had a heart attack in 1958 she rushed to his bedside and nursed him through his illness. Soon after when she needed surgery for kidney stones, he looked after her most tenderly. They also went on a fun holiday to Srinagar with their boys. In 1960 Feroze suffered another heart attack. A massive one this time. Though Indira sat by his bed through the night willing him to pull through, he eventually passed away. For the third time in her life Indira was faced with the loss of someone whom she had loved intensely. 'It was as though someone had cut me in two,' she said later. (*Mother India by* Pranay Gupte).

Rae Bareli

Seventy kilometres from Lucknow, the state capital of UP, is Rae Bareli. Originally founded by the Bhars, it soon became the stronghold of the Kayasthas. Their title 'Rai' was prefixed to Bareli and it has remained Rae Bareli ever since. Feroze Gandhi in 1951 stood for the first general elections from here and won handsomely. He was returned a second time in 1957. After him, his wife Indira chose to stand for elections from there in 1967 (won), 1971 (won but declared invalid), 1977 (lost) and then again in 1980 (won). Indira gave up the Rae Bareli seat to Arun Nehru, a member of the Nehru family, in 1980. Twenty years after Indira's death, her daughter-in-law Sonia, Rajiv's widow, stood from Rae Bareli in 2004 for the first time and won. She won handsomely again from there in the 2009 elections as well. Today Rae Bareli continues to be a Nehru-Gandhi stronghold.

Indira was shattered. The couple had known each other for so long, gone through so much together personally and politically that she just couldn't accept the fact that Feroze was no more. They had been living apart it was true, but now that he was gone she felt a deep void. She wrote to Rajiv who was back at school in Dehradun, 'The first . . . days I was quite numb, and although my eyes were aching and burning I could not really cry. But now I have begun to cry and don't seem able to stop.'(*Indira* by Katherine Frank)

Politics now became even more important to her.

She had taken her first few steps into the national arena in 1955 by becoming a member of the Congress Working Committee. Then she became the president of the All India Youth Congress. After that as a member of the Allahabad Election Congress Committee she was soon elected to the Congress Central Committee. She very quickly proved that she had some of her mother's feminist genes. Indira revamped the women's wing of the Congress and began speaking out on women's issues. By 1959 she was elected unopposed as president of the Indian National Congress itself, a post her grandfather and her father had held before her. Jawaharlal Nehru was happy for her. Indira was now in her own right, a part of the political system.

Indira quickly showed she could be an astute and practical politician. Kerala had a democratically elected Communist Party government. She helped topple it. By getting people out on the streets to agitate, her party created a law and order situation. She then called for President's Rule in Kerala, claiming the Communist Party had lost control of the situation. President's Rule was thus enforced, the Communist Party was made to step down and Kerala was brought under the centre. Her father was dismayed at the way it was done and the events did cause a lot of public consternation. But Indira's efforts paid off when in the subsequent election the Congress-led coalition won.

Soon another occasion to display her political acumen presented itself. India on attaining independence had been reorganized into states on linguistic lines. Bombay was the capital of the bilingual Bombay Presidency which included both Maharashtra and Gujarat. Now both regions wanted separate identities and laid claim to Bombay as their capital. Riots broke out. Indira swiftly recommended separating both territories. Bombay was given to Maharashtra and the agitation was put to an end before it spiralled out of control.

Slowly the shy, retiring introvert who was her father's political shadow was finding her feet. She was coming into her own as an assertive and self-confident politician.

But even before her two-year term as Congress President got over, she stepped down saying she was unwell. This could be true because her health right from her childhood had always been a problem. There was even a suspicion that she might have had TB in the past just like her mother. Even so that didn't stop her from continuing with her social work or looking after her father.

Then in the October of 1962, China, long considered a trusted friend by Jawaharlal Nehru, attacked India. They overran large areas of the North-east and Jammu and Kashmir and withdrew after totally annihilating the Indian army. But Indira in a confidence-building measure bravely flew to Tezpur just thirty miles from where the Chinese were and even went on air for a radio broadcast. Little more than a year later Nehru, who had never really got over the shock of the Chinese incursion, suffered his first stroke. He became a shadow of his former self and Indira found him depending more and more on her. She had always put her father's needs before hers so now she not only saw to his personal wants— giving him his medicines and so on—but also began criss-crossing the world on his behalf and representing him at various international conferences.

On 27 May 1964, seventeen years after he first became prime minister, Jawaharlal Nehru slipped into a coma and passed away. His death left his daughter distraught and the nation in despair. In a daze Indira, clad in white, sat by her father's body as millions of grieving people filed past. Then following in an open jeep while helicopters scattered rose petals, she saw yet another sea of weeping humanity line the entire route to Shantivana on the banks of the River Jamuna where he was to be cremated. As Rajiv, who was studying in the UK, couldn't get back in time, eighteen-year-old Sanjay lit the pyre. Thirteen days later and twenty-eight years after Kamala's death, Indira immersed her father's ashes along with her mother's—kept by his bedside all these years—in the Ganges and scattered the rest all over India, just as he had wanted.

Indira now slipped into a sort of depression.

The question of 'after Nehru who?' began to make the rounds. Indira was asked if she would assume leadership. She refused. So a unanimously chosen Lal Bahadur Shastri became the prime minister of the country. Teen Murti House was turned into a memorial-museum and Indira was required to move out. She was now offered the foreign minister's post. Still grieving, she refused once again, but Shastri was insistent. He wanted Nehru's daughter in his cabinet. However, to become a minister Indira needed to win an election, which she hadn't. The other option was, she could be offered a ministry by being nominated to the Rajya Sabha. So that is what they did, and she reluctantly became the minister for Information and Broadcasting. Indira was now allotted 1 Safdarjang Road, a house where she was to reside for the next twenty-odd years.

Her leadership qualities soon came involuntarily to the fore. When anti-Hindi protestors went on the rampage in Madras, it was Indira who without hesitation air-dashed to pacify the agitators. And around the same time in 1965 when Pakistan tried to capture Kashmir for the second time, Indira again was first on the scene in Kashmir to provide moral support to the Indian troops. India defeated Pakistan and a ceasefire was declared. But as Russia was brokering a peace pact between India and Pakistan, Prime Minister Shastri went on a visit to Tashkent. He died suddenly of a heart attack there. Within a few weeks of his death Indira emerged as the consensus candidate to succeed Shastri.

The stage was now set for her next avatar.

Architect of Modern India

Jawaharlal Nehru was India's first prime minister and was at the helm of affairs for seventeen years. He had not only fought shoulder to shoulder with Gandhiji to achieve India's independence but had also laid the foundation of a modern India. He created the Planning Commission to tackle India's economic, rural, medical, education issues through regular Five Year Plans (we are currently in the 12th plan). These plans set up the IITs, the All India Institute of Medical Sciences, the University Grants Commission (education), etc. Many small and large-scale industries like the Bhilai Steel Plant came up while dams like the Bhakra Nangal were also commissioned. Nehru oversaw India's foreign policy and was greatly appreciated for his role in world politics. He was one of the founding members of the famous Non-Aligned Movement where member countries like India, Yugoslavia, Indonesia, and Egypt would remain neutral in case of a war or any disagreement between the major powers. His Panch Sheel or the five principles of peaceful coexistence with China was at that time hailed as a path-breaking initiative. But unfortunately China didn't adhere to it. Jawaharlal Nehru was an idealist who truly believed in the principles of sovereignty, democracy and secularism. Almost every institution we have today is a result of his forethought and hope for a prosperous and independent India.

Affectionately known as Pandit (Scholar) Nehru, he was a handsome man always dressed impeccably in achkan and churidars with a red rose in his buttonhole. His jacket is famous the world over as the Nehru Jacket just like Gandhiji's topi (cap) is known as the Gandhi Topi today. Nehru spent nine years of his life in jail, the longest spell being three years in the Ahmadnagar jail— He was president of the Congress Party for six terms. He spent his time in jail, writing. His works include: *The Discovery of India, Glimpses of World History, An Autobiography* and *Letters from a Father to His Daughter.* His birthday, 14th of November, is celebrated as Children's Day across India when youngsters remember 'Chacha Nehru' with affection.

15   It's a Girl!

Indira was excited but outwardly calm. In a white khadi sari and a brown shawl, a string of brown beads round her neck she stood silently in front of her father's portrait at Teen Murti House just as she had at Gandhiji's Samadhi a few minutes earlier. It was then time for her to head for Parliament House. It was the 19th of January 1966. With Shastri's sudden demise, less than two years after Jawaharlal Nehru's death, Congress Party was once again gathering to vote for a new leader.

Indira knew her name was up for election. She also knew that the 'Syndicate' or the coterie (group) headed by Kamaraj, the Congress Party President, was quietly sponsoring her candidature not because they liked her or believed she was capable of being a good leader but because they disliked her opponent Morarji Desai more. They also thought that as Nehru's daughter, the nation would gladly accept her but importantly she was young, inexperienced and therefore malleable.

Her performance as the Information and Broadcasting Minister had been unremarkable and as a parliamentarian she was worse. She could in fact barely hold her own. So the Syndicate assumed they would be able to control and rule through her. Morarji Desai on the other hand was stern, authoritarian and rather unpopular. His plans to become prime minister had been thwarted once already when the Syndicate had forced him into withdrawing his candidature in order to make Shastri the unanimous choice. But this time round he was unwilling to pull out even through the Syndicate once again was determined to scuttle his chances.

People began to gather outside Parliament House even as 526 Congress Party members of Parliament within began casting their votes. Indira and Morarji Desai did not vote. Four hours later the chief whip of the party came out. 'It's a girl' he announced dramatically to the waiting crowd. Indira Gandhi had trounced Desai by 355 to 169 votes. She first thanked the members for electing her. Next she strode up to a morose Morarji Desai and asked for his blessings. And to jubilant cries of 'Indira Gandhi Zindabad' drove home to savour her victory. She then went to the President to stake her claim to form the new government. She was forty-nine years old.

Rashtrapati Bhavan was teeming with members of Parliament as one by one the invitees came in. The swearing-in ceremony was to take place in the magnificent Ashoka Hall. A podium with two microphones faced rows of chairs one behind the other. It was the same hall where her father had been sworn in nineteen years ago. As Indira arrived to take her place, an excited sigh ran through the crowd. President S. Radhakrishnan arrived and everyone stood up. The national anthem was played and the President beckoned

Indira to step forward. In a shy, almost apprehensive voice she raised her right hand and took the oath of office: 'I Indira Gandhi do solemnly affirm that I will bear true faith and allegiance to the Constitution of India as by law established, that I will uphold the sovereignty and integrity of India, that I will conscientiously discharge my duties as prime minister for the Union and that I will do right to all manner of people in accordance with the Constitution and the law, without fear or favour, affection or ill will.'

Indira Gandhi thus became independent India's first woman prime minister. She was now not only the head of one of the world's largest democracies, she was also according to the *Time* magazine at the helm of a 'troubled India'. India at that time was steeped in poverty. She also faced severe drought, food shortages, famines, inflation and even regional agitations.

Initially Indira struggled, especially in Parliament. Not a good speaker she was ineffective in the House and was constantly heckled. Much to everyone's amusement but her own annoyance she was even called a 'goongi gudiya' (dumb doll) by the opposition. But slowly and steadily, outside Parliament she began to take matters into her own hands and as she gained in confidence she began asserting herself. She chose her own advisers and experts—those she could trust—to guide her.

Faced with the uphill task of tackling a tottering economy she took tough measures, some popular, some not.

First, devalue the rupee, her advisers told her. Devaluation simply means lowering the worth of a country's currency against the currencies of other countries. It is generally done to help create favourable market conditions. All countries do it sometime or the other. By devaluing or weakening the rupee, Indira hoped to receive more foreign aid and food shipments from abroad because it would make it cheaper for them. It would also buy her some time for introducing other measures to make India more self-reliant.

However, it caused a nationwide furore. Even Kamaraj and the Congress Working Committee opposed the move. Nevertheless she went ahead with it. She showed them she was quite capable of taking tough decisions and combating opposition—even from her own party men.

Next she tackled the food crisis. She managed to tide over the initial difficulties by convincing the US to send in massive amounts of wheat through the PL480 program. But this supply was very erratic. So she looked for other avenues and building on the reforms started by her father and Lal Bahadur Shastri, encouraged the Green Revolution.

The Green Revolution has an interesting history. It is a programme of seeding developed by a Norman Borlaug of the US. After the Second World War, a US agriculturist working in Japan discovered 'Norin', a unique kind of wheat grain. He sent it to the US for research and breeding. After thirteen years of experimenting, a new wheat seed called 'Gaines' was created. Norman Borlaug experimented further and crossed this with a Mexican wheat seed. And to his joy it resulted in a seed that could not only grow in abundance but was inexpensive as well.

Now due to droughts, famines as well as the British policies of the past, India's food shortage was acute. People were starving and dying by the thousands. So M.S. Swaminathan, an eminent Indian agricultural scientist, decided to try it out in India. These seeds were sown in a small patch of ground in Pusa. The results were spectacular. So 18,000 tonnes of these seeds were imported and planted in the Punjab. Production increased tremendously and India in less than three years became more than self-sufficient in food production. Similar hybrid varieties of rice and other crops were introduced. Yields increased. And soon India began exporting as well.

Operation Flood was soon to follow. Verghese Kurien pioneered the world's largest co-operative dairy development programme in Anand, Gujarat and milk production increased dramatically. Kurien soon came to be known as the Father of the White Revolution and the Milkman of India. He also introduced us to the highly popular 'utterly butterly delicious Amul!'

The Punjab, an issue festering since Independence, also needed attention. The Sikhs had first wanted a separate homeland and then when India was divided into states on linguistic lines, they demanded a separate state. They got neither. But it caused a divide between Hindi-speaking Punjabis and the Punjabi-speaking

Sikhs. The agitation, militant at times, continued with the clamour for separation refusing to die down. So Indira split the Punjab into three states—Haryana, Himachal Pradesh and Punjab. Haryana and Punjab were now forced to share Chandigarh as their capital. The Sikhs were not happy.

The1967 general elections were around the corner. Indira Gandhi knew she needed to firm up her position as a national leader on her own and not as a figure propped up by the Syndicate. In any case the entire so-called Syndicate was now totally hostile towards her. Therefore she needed to be elected directly by the people. So for the first time she stood for the Lok Sabha elections. Not from her father's constituency Phulpur in UP, which now belonged to her aunt Vijayalakshmi, but from Rae Bareli, her husband Feroze's constituency. In a rare gesture her aunt told her, 'You can stand from Phulpur if you like,' but Indira gracefully refused.

Campaigning extensively throughout India she tried to connect with the people. Exhibiting great courage even after her nose was fractured by a stone thrown at her, she continued to campaign, bandaged and bleeding. She reminded them of her background and told them how from her very childhood the people of India had been her family. 'My burden is manifold because,' she said, 'crores of my family members are poverty-stricken and I have to look after them. (*Indira* by Katherine Frank).

The Constitution of India

The Constitution of India is a framework of guidelines, rules and principles by which the country is governed. It came into effect on 26 January 1950, the same day Purna Swaraj had been declared earlier in 1930. The constitution declares India to be a sovereign, socialist, secular, democratic Republic. It is the longest constitution in the world.

The Parliament consists of two houses—the Rajya Sabha or the upper house consisting of 250 members, and the Lok Sabha or the lower house consisting of 545 members. Members of each house are elected and they represent constituents or citizens/voters who live in a particular state. There are twenty-eight states and seven union territories in India. Legislative/General elections are held every five years. The party that wins a two-thirds majority comes to power and chooses the prime minister. But if no party achieves the required majority, then parties may form a coalition with other parties to achieve a majority and form a government just like we have today.

If any Article in the Constitution is to be amended or changed, it is put to vote in the Lok Sabha as well as the Rajya Sabha and has to be passed by both houses with a two-thirds majority.

16   Not a Smooth Ride

Indira Gandhi romped home to a massive victory personally, but many of the Syndicate were defeated and the Congress could manage only a bare majority. However, Morarji Desai did win and though this time there was no doubt about who was going to be prime minister, she had to accept Desai as her deputy. He was also given the finance portfolio. Indira was now determined to brook no interference from the Syndicate.

Announcing a ten point anti-poverty programme in 1967, she began pushing her measures through. And every step she took was severely criticized. The Syndicate shouted louder than the rest. Wherever possible she also began to bring non-Congress state governments under President's Rule, which meant under the Centre or technically her rule. Indira was being practical. In order to push through her various reforms she needed them under her control. So by methods that were not always acceptable she was slowly but surely increasing her hold. This naturally began to annoy the old coterie headed by Desai.

Indira always remained extremely concerned about the poor, and despite her privileged background was at heart a socialist. Socialism broadly means programmes for the benefit of society as a whole—usually government driven. So 'Nationalization' was one of the reforms on her agenda. It meant bringing various industries under the government's control. She wanted to nationalize the banks first because she felt she could then introduce various schemes to help the underprivileged: to get loans and enable savings which the poor couldn't till now.

Desai as finance minister, however, was opposed to it. It also first needed to be passed in Parliament and she wasn't sure it would. So overnight she summarily took away the finance portfolio from him and then instead of sending the bill to Parliament got the President to issue an ordinance (order) nationalizing the banks—fourteen of them—which was technically not incorrect. Desai resigned and Indira was happy to accept his resignation. It was a hugely popular measure with the general public. But within the year, in 1970, the Supreme Court struck this ordinance down as unconstitutional since it hadn't been passed in Parliament.

The same thing happened to her proposal for the abolition of 'privy purses and privileges' to princes. India before Independence had consisted of many princely states loosely held together under the British rule. With Independence many of these princes, like the Maharajas of Mysore, Gwalior, etc., opted to join the Indian Union. Certain privileges and a fixed amount of money depending on their size and importance were promised to them. This Indira felt was draining the government treasury of a huge amount of wealth that could be put to better use. But this amendment to the Constitution put before Parliament was defeated in the Rajya Sabha by one vote, although it had been passed by the Lok Sabha. So she again got the President to issue a Presidential Ordinance to derecognize the princes and abolish their purses and privileges. Once again popular with the people, the Supreme Court turned it down the same year for the same reason.

Before that when the then President Zakir Hussain died suddenly, Indira opponents in the Congress seized the opportunity to try and make Sanjiva Reddy, one of their own, the next President. Indira realized he could be used against her, perhaps even to unseat her. The prime minister once elected is appointed by the President, so technically he has the right to dismiss her too if necessary. So although she formally nominated Sanjiva Reddy as the Congress Party candidate, his opponent Vice President V.V. Giri won. It was rumoured that Indira had subtly engineered his victory. The old stalwarts were furious and within weeks met to expel her from the party for 'indiscipline and defiance of party leadership'. (*Indira* by Katherine Frank). The year was 1969.

She was deeply hurt. 'Nobody,' she said angrily, 'can throw me out of the Congress,' a party of which she had been a part of since infancy. She also knew if she accepted the expulsion she would no longer be party president and therefore no longer prime minister, since usually it is the party president who is made prime minister. She called for a split. More than half the congressmen swore loyalty to her and her party became the Requisition (Ruling) Congress(R) while the rest of the Syndicate became the Organization (Old) Congress (O). However, she lost her majority. Friendly non-Congress parties now extended their support to her so that her minority government wouldn't fall and she could remain prime minister.

But Indira was beginning to feel completely frustrated. She was finding it difficult to get any proposal through—either in Parliament where her party now didn't have complete majority or by the judiciary. There were even rumours of an army coup to overthrow her. She decided she needed to do something about it. If she was to govern without fear she needed complete control. And that could only be obtained by going to the people once again.

She decided to call for midterm elections in 1971 instead of waiting for the next year, as scheduled. Now it was not the party she asked people to vote for, but for her—'Indira'—a symbol of progress. She went from village to village covering more than 35,000 miles and addressing over 250 public meetings, and as against the opposition's 'Indira Hatao' asked people to vote for her to 'Garibi Hatao'. Her speeches were now greatly improved and full of grand passion.

Finally at home after a hard campaign and surrounded by her family and friends Indira awaited the results. She was not disappointed. Result after result went in favour of the Congress (R). Indira could hardly contain her delight. She herself had soundly thrashed her opponent Raj Narain in Rae Bareli. Excited party workers began dropping in. Sweets and flowers were distributed. This time round she had won even more comprehensively with two-thirds majority. Congress (O) was completely routed.

Placing India on the World Map

Indira's foreign policy was dictated by what Indira felt were the needs of her country. She first represented India at the 1964 Commonwealth Heads of Government Meeting. Then as prime minister in 1966 she followed it up with a tour of France, US, UK, USSR, Yugoslavia and UAE where she explained what she saw was India's role in relation to the rest of the world. Sri Lanka and the golden jubilee celebrations of the 1917 Russian Revolution in Moscow were next on her itinerary. In 1968 she visited Bhutan, Singapore, Australia, New Zealand, Malaysia, Brazil, Chile, Argentina and Venezuela and then was invited to address the General Assembly of the UN.

A year later she spoke at the silver jubilee session of the UN too. Slowly India was finding her place in the world. Signing a twenty-year treaty of friendship and co-operation with the USSR, she ensured continued Soviet support. However, despite shared ideals she wasn't quite as successful with the US. In 1972, addressing the UN and the World Health Assembly, she called on the affluent countries to work for improving the environment and removing diseases. When at the seventh Non-Aligned Summit Meet Indira took over as chairperson from Fidel Castro of Cuba, India was recognized officially as an emerging world power. India was now no longer seen as a country steeped in poverty but a proud developing nation who not only stood for peace and mutual co-operation but one who was willing to play her role as a leader of other developing countries.

17 A Feisty Leader

Indira Gandhi was now cresting a hugely popular personal wave. She no longer needed the party. She was the party. Her popularity cut across all regional and communal divides and she believed she had the permission of the nation to embark on any form of legislative reform. She also now had the required majority in Parliament to vote through whatever reform she wanted. So she began ammending the constitution often. This was a dangerous precedent because the constitution of any country is considered sacrosanct and shouldn't normally be tampered with.

First she deprived the princes of their purses and privileges once and for all. She then nationalized the insurance and coal industries without much ado. Next she ensured that any changes she may bring about in the Fundamental Rights of the people would not be set aside by the judiciary. For good measure she also introduced a rather repressive security act MISA which allowed people to be arrested and imprisoned without trial for up to a year.

By doing all this Indira believed she was upholding the 'rights of the largest number of people', i.e. the democracy. But according to her critics she was steadily weakening the great institutions on which Indian democracy rested. She even advocated a complete overhaul of the Constitution 'in the interests of the people', but thankfully that did not happen. Even so many intellectuals accused her of 'reducing the Constitution to tatters'.

Trouble, however, soon broke out in neighbouring East Pakistan. When India was partitioned into two, the Pakistan that was newly created consisted of two unconnected parts separated by more than a thousand miles of Indian territory which included areas of East Bengal. This was known as East Pakistan. Now due to cultural differences and neglect by West Pakistan, the easterners led by Sheikh Mujibur Rahman went on a civil disobedience movement, asking for greater regional independence. Pakistani President Yahya Khan took severe measures against this movement. It resulted in thousands of East Pakistanis fleeing across the borders into India. They came in such large numbers that Indira realized India would not be able to sustain them for long as the country did not have the resources to look after so many refugees. Nevertheless the Indian government not only helped feed and clothe them but also sheltered them in numerous camps, all the while training and arming the Mukti Bahini (the Bangladesh–East Pakistan) liberation army as well.

Indira was worried. She had appealed to all the world leaders and even toured extensively across the globe to build awareness about Yahya Khan's reign of terror and India's inability to cope with the refugees.

But while the Soviet Union was sympathetic, the US warned her against going to war with Pakistan. The US Seventh Fleet even sailed threateningly into the Bay of Bengal. So Indira defiantly went on a whirlwind trip to the remotest outposts of the Indian defence to shore up their confidence in preparation for battle. And as the hype on war got louder and louder Pakistan believed India might indeed attack her. So on 3 December 1971, hoping to catch her by surprise, Pakistan made an all out assault on India, on the western sector in Kashmir. Indian troops repulsed the attack magnificently. The Indians not only notched up stupendous victories in the west but also marched into East Pakistan and forced the Pakistani General Niazi to surrender unconditionally. This action effectively gave birth to a new nation—Bangladesh.

It was Indira's finest hour. Cheering crowds welcomed her everywhere. Even the ever critical members of Parliament gave her a standing ovation. While all of India beamed with pride, it heralded her arrival on the world arena as a strong defender of human rights. In Pakistan, the defeated military government collapsed and within six months Zulfikar Ali Bhutto, the new President of Pakistan, came to Simla to sign the 1972 Simla Accord with Indira. Although she lost the opportunity to make the line of control a permanent border, it was agreed that henceforth India and Pakistan would solve the Kashmir issue through discussions only and not by war; nor would anybody else be allowed to intervene. Later she came up with a six point Kashmir Accord in Parliament to confirm Kashmir's position as an integral part of India with special status.

Soon, trouble started brewing in Sikkim—an independent Indian protectorate state on the Indo-Tibetan border—against its monarch, the Chogyal. The situation demanded Indira's attention. Ignoring the Chogyal's appeals, in 1974 she promptly sent in troops to make Sikkim the 22nd state of the Indian Union. Why? In the interest of upholding democratic ideals, of course. It was a smart move. It created a much-needed buffer zone between India and China.

Indira now wondered how to make India a strong global power. It could only be through the development of science and technology. And one fine morning the world was shocked to find that India had become the sixth nuclear power in the world. A nuclear test for purely peaceful purposes was conducted at Pokharan in Rajasthan (1974). Code-named 'Smiling Buddha' it not only enhanced Indira's image at home and abroad, it also put India firmly among the elite nations of the world.

Aryabhata the first Indian space satellite's successful launch was to follow. Then about ten years later the nation watched proudly as Squadron Leader Rakesh Sharma, India's first man in space, from a Soviet Space station Salyut 7 told a smiling Indira that from space India indeed was 'Sare Jahan se achha'. Indira also felt that India's communication and defence technologies needed to be upgraded so she created a powerful intelligence gathering bureau that could quickly identify threats from within the country and outside.

In the sixth Five Year Plan, she worked out a whole programme for women's education and development. But by merely being herself women began seeing her as a role model. And like the time when she helped fit a set of artificial legs to a boy who had lost them during the Partition riots and set up the first Bal Bhavan and Bal Sahayog for children, she actually pioneered childcare in India. In practically every field as far-ranging as healthcare to sports or to mountaineering, she successfully set up departments to help people.

Despite her successes, it was not a peaceful period for Indira.

Kashmir

At the time of the Partition in 1947 there were 562 Princely States in India. They were asked to opt for India or Pakistan. Now the state of Jammu and Kashmir had a predominantly Muslim population but was ruled by Maharaja Hari Singh, a Hindu king. While he was dithering about whom to join, Pakistani tribals launched an attack to liberate 'Muslim' Kashmir from a 'Hindu' Raja. Unnerved, Hari Singh asked Delhi for help and joined the Indian union by which time the Pakistani tribals had already occupied large areas of Kashmir. And before the Indian army could push them out completely, Pandit Nehru appealed to the UN to intervene.

So the UN declared an immediate ceasefire. Pakistan was asked to vacate the occupied regions and agree to a plebiscite, according to which the people would vote to decide whether they wanted to become part of Pakistan or remain with India. But Pakistan would not vacate and so no plebiscite was held. As a result 35 per cent of Kashmir is occupied by Pakistan while 45 per cent remains with India. 20 per cent is with China after China annexed it in the 1962 war.

In 1965 Pakistan tried to capture Indian Kashmir again. This time India threw them back. With Russia's intervention, the Tashkent Agreement was signed agreeing to a ceasefire. In 1971 Pakistan attacked India again, and this time they were defeated so soundly that the country split into two. Bangladesh came into being.

Then Pakistan began to slyly send in hundreds of militants to create violence and terrorist attacks not only in Kashmir but across India. In 1999 when the Indian army retreated from the line of control for the winter as they usually do, Pakistan crossed the LOC and occupied the Kargil ranges which overlook the highway connecting Ladakh and Srinagar. They hoped to cut off Ladakh from Kashmir. The Indian army gave them another sound hiding and reclaimed all occupied peaks.

But Pakistan has still not given up. The clandestine warfare still continues.

18   A Basketful of Woes

Indira landslide victory had won her a huge mandate. The 1971 war had cemented her position. She appeared invincible. But she was soon disillusioned. Inflation, unemployment, food shortages—despite the Green Revolution—and sudden droughts were causing strikes and riots across the nation. And instead of helping, her opponents were constantly accusing her of being authoritarian and dictatorial. 'Could there be anyone in the country who was more committed to the people of the country than I am?' she wondered disappointedly. In fact every step she took and every amendment she pushed through was in the interests of the people. Yet they suspected her motives.

They called the Congress a party of 'Indira loyalists'. Perhaps. But weren't her cabinet ministers all good men? Her advisers too, like her principal private secretary, P.N. Haksar, were experts in their field and brilliant officers. But yes she certainly wasn't prepared to brook any unnecessary opposition. She had been elected prime minister to look after the interests of the people of India hadn't she? So she needed committed people who could carry out whatever was necessary to improve the life of the common man.

That is probably why when a case on the legality of the government's (her) right to make Constitutional Amendments came up in the Supreme Court and the judgement was not to her liking, she superseded those judges and appointed a junior judge as Chief Justice over them. The superseded judges resigned and this caused a nationwide outcry.

The prime minister's office too became increasingly proactive in every field, including fundraising or collecting money for the party. Sycophancy and corruption began to flourish. Though Indira herself lived very sparingly and economically she was now seen to support a group of people who couldn't care less how things were done—by crookery or dishonesty—just so long as it was done. The unselfish ideals of party and country that had won India her independence were, everyone was quick to point out, being slowly eroded. Indira's popularity therefore began to plummet.

To add to her woes, there was also a large section of growing rebels determined to make matters worse for her. It was headed by an old Gandhian Jayaprakash Narayan, a friend and contemporary of her father. His wife Prabha had been Kamala Nehru's best friend. The JP movement, as it came to be known, started in Bihar but soon assumed threatening proportions. Unhappy with Indira's rule JP asked people—farmers, landless labourers and the middle class—across the country to join hands, strike work and remove her. A nationwide railway strike was also called late. So Indira began ruthlessly putting down strikes, arresting people and sending them to jail. This only made matters worse. More and more people began joining the movement.

Around this time a petition filed by Raj Narain, her opponent in the 1971 elections, accusing Indira of election malpractice came up for hearing in the Allahabad court before Justice J.M.L Sinha. He upheld it. He agreed that (Yashpal Kapoor), one of her election agents, had not yet resigned from the government when he started working as her representative. The election rules state that no government servant while still in service could work as a candidate's election agent. So though the overlap was of a mere week the judge held Indira Gandhi's election invalid. She was debarred for six years. That technicality set the cat among the pigeons. Indira was required to step down. As far as she was concerned this was the last straw. She suspected a conspiracy brewing against her.

When JP, rallying his followers to march to Delhi, called out to the army and the police to mutiny and overthrow her, Indira felt threatened. She invoked Article 352 of the Constitution whereby in the event of a threat to India's security—internal or external—the President could suspend the Constitution temporarily and impose Emergency in the country. So since, according to Indira, the country was in 'a state of anarchy', she went to President Fakhruddin Ali Ahmed and asked him to declare Emergency. The President did so. And India was now technically brought under President's Rule. But as it was customary for the President to always listen to and act on the prime minister's advice, the entire country was now more or less in Indira's sole control. The police soon swooped down on all the leaders of the JP movement, arrested them and threw them into jail. JP with other high-profile celebrities found himself behind bars. The media was suppressed and censorship imposed.

Indira then in an emotion-packed speech told her nation that 'a climate of violence and hatred had been created . . . opposition parties were working to destabilize the country . . . one of them went to the extent of saying that armed forces would not carry out orders . . . this had to be prevented . . . so to safeguard and preserve Indian democracy . . .' (*Indira* by Katherine Frank) she proclaimed that she had no option but to declare Emergency.

Then with the Emergency in force Indira announced a twenty point economic programme. It aimed at helping the poor and the middle class. For instance, most villages had something called bonded labour where for generations people of a family had to work for a particular landlord in order to pay off their debts. She made this practice illegal and cancelled all the debts of the poor. Similarly there were other measures which were truly beneficial and under the Emergency conditions improved for the Indian citizen in many ways. But Indira was nevertheless accused of misuse of power.

Now just before the declaration of Emergency in 1975 her younger son Sanjay, newly returned from the UK, had begun creating waves. Without any qualification other than a minor apprenticeship at the Rolls-Royce Motor Cars Ltd UK, he had demanded and obtained a license for starting a car factory in Haryana. But the Maruti car he produced turned out to be a dud. The project never really took off despite rules being bent and funds raised illegally to help Sanjay.

Sanjay was a young man in a hurry. He apparently had scant respect for rules, regulations or even honesty, and Indira seemed unable or unwilling to stop him. Without informing his mother he also involved himself in many unsavoury deals. And when her trusted lieutenant P.N. Haksar warned her about Sanjay's wrongdoings, instead of taking her son to task, Indira quietly sacked Haksar. Wary of people since her childhood, Indira, now faced with the constant criticism of Sanjay, became even more suspicious and distrustful. She believed plots were afoot to destroy her. So she began to depend heavily on Sanjay. And with the declaration of Emergency, he swung into action with even more verve.

Sanjay came up with a programme to improve conditions in the country. This not only caused his mother's downfall but hastened it. It was a laudable programme but unfortunately its execution was not. It took a while for Indira to realize that her son's activities were causing widespread unrest and hostility. That it was turning the nation against her and forcing the members of her party to defect. So to minimize the damage Indira decided that elections would be held on schedule in 1976. But Sanjay convinced her to postpone it not once but twice. In March 1977 Indira finally took matters into her own hands and announced immediate elections. She stood again from Rae Bareli. Sanjay filed his papers in neighbouring Amethi.

After a gruelling campaign, a visibly tired Indira was home. For the first time in her political career she had sensed a certain kind of public hostility towards her. People across India in the past had always welcomed her like a long-lost daughter, but this time she had been shouted down and even booed at. Now apprehensively she awaited the results.

She soon heard that she was trailing her old opponent Raj Narain. Her friend Pupul Jayakar dropped by to be with her. So did Rajiv and Sonia. Sanjay was away in Lucknow. No one was in any mood to talk and they sat together in grim silence. The atmosphere was completely different from the previous occasions when they had assembled to await election results. They were toying with their dinner when the news they feared came in. Indira had lost. Sanjay too. Ministers now began to arrive. Most of them had been defeated. The Congress (R) was in fact completely decimated. The Janata Party led alliance had won. It was well past midnight by the time everybody left and she wearily turned in for the night.

Two days later, showing great grace and dignity in defeat, Indira went to the acting President B.D. Jatti as Fakhruddin Ali Ahmed had in the in the meanwhile died of a heart attack. Twenty-one months after she had asked for Emergency, Indira requested that it be lifted. She also submitted her resignation. She had been prime minister for eleven years. With her old foes now firmly in command the new foreign minister Atal

Bihari Vajpayi was quick to say, 'The Janata Party would consign Indira Gandhi to the dustbin of history.' (*Indira* by Katherine Frank).

Little did he know.

A Parallel Power Base

With already a reputation for getting into trouble, Sanjay Gandhi was just twenty-two when he began making his presence felt in India. As the prime minister's son he soon had a coterie of young supporters who owed allegiance only to him. When the Raj Narain case came back to haunt his mother, he came into his own. He began advising her on all matters including apparently the declaration of Emergency. He soon had a parallel power centre working from the prime minister's house.

He began interfering in the running of the government and even controlling ministerial appointments and ministries. Those who opposed him were ruthlessly punished. He revived the Youth Congress to help him carry out a five point programme to tackle the population problem, beautify the cities, abolish dowry, improve literacy (each one teach one), and end the caste system. All creditable ideas, but the manner in which they were carried out only caused his mother's downfall. His family-planning drives forcibly sterilized lakhs of people. His demolition squads equipped with bulldozers mercilessly removed slums and encroachments to clear and widen roads. He levelled large areas of unhygienic and insanitary tenements. But they were all heavily populated and Sanjay soon became disliked by all.

19   Mixed Fortunes

Indira Gandhi knew they would be coming to arrest her soon. After all, hadn't she put most of them in jail during the Emergency? So why would they show her any compassion now?

They had already forced her to move out of 1 Safdarjang Road, knowing she had no home to go to. Anand Bhawan, her erstwhile home in Allahabad, had already been donated to the nation and was now a museum. So for the first time in her life Indira—personally—had not only no job or money (except for royalties from her father's books), she also had no home of her own.

Mohammad Yunus, an old family friend, came to her rescue. He offered her his house. And so she moved into 12 Willingdon Crescent with her two sons and their families. The new Janata Party led government headed by her old foe, the eighty-one-year-old Morarji Desai, who had finally realized his dream of becoming prime minister, was looking for ways and means to humiliate her. Though there were better residences available, Desai determined to make life difficult for her had insisted he wanted Indira's. He had reduced her security as well.

And so, as expected the men from the Central Bureau of Investigation (CBI) came for her. Indira made no fuss. She was taken to the Delhi Police Lines and locked up. She spent the night quietly reading. Next day she was produced before the magistrate. She was charged with making money out of selling jeeps to the army and with signing a contract with a French oil company whose bid was higher than all other bids. But the magistrate threw the case out and released her unconditionally. Result: Indira Gandhi emerged a martyr who was unnecessarily being hounded by the Janata Party.

But that was not all. Her passport, along with those of her family, was impounded. Their phones were tapped and they were tailed. The various government departments including the Income Tax began to harass them. Sanjay was arrested and then freed on bail. Books demonising her began to appear on the stands and hate articles started to make the rounds.

Under Justice Shah, a commission was set up to look into her misdemeanours during the Emergency. It was a highly publicized affair. Indira was ordered to present herself before the commission. But Shah was openly biased against her. 'I am not bound legally or constitutionally to reply,' she told him when he persisted in asking her humiliating questions. The Shah Commission Report soundly indicted her but it eventually failed to make any real impact. So Special Courts were set up to try her and Sanjay. Twenty-eight criminal cases were filed against her alone.

Now Indira's many so-called friends began avoiding her. Her party split a second time in 1978 into Congress (I), I for Indira, and Congress (S), S for Swaran Singh. This time, only seventy members stuck by her. The 'hand' became her new party symbol. Though the Janata Party government did undo some of her Emergency measures, they spent more time trying to discredit and demean her rather than govern the country. But she conducted herself with such dignity and poise through this entire witch-hunt that the nation began to look upon her more as the victim of a vindictive Janata Party government rather than the evil oppressor of the Emergency.

In between all this, Indira went to JP and made her peace with him. He forgave her instantly. But before that a horrendous massacre of Harijans took place in Belchi, an inaccessible village in Bihar. Even before the Janata Party could react, Indira travelled by train, jeep and tractor, through mud, slush and floods and even on elephant back to offer them succour. The demoralized and frightened villagers greeted her as they would a liberator. As a result, feeling more confident she visited her constituency Rae Bareli. She was once more welcomed like a long-lost daughter. People appeared to have forgiven her. Using the opportunity to apologize for the excesses of the Emergency she also began to denounce the Janata Party. Wherever she went people now flocked to see her. She was slowly regaining her connect with the masses.

And then when she embarked on a whirlwind tour of the South, thousands turned up to welcome their

'Indira amma'. Therefore Indira decided to chance her luck at a by-election from Chikmaglur in Karnataka. She trounced her Janata Party opponent. This so rattled the Janata Party that they now charged her with having obstructed officials in an ongoing investigation of Sanjay's Maruti Company. They not only expelled her from Parliament for contempt but also shockingly sent her to prison again.

It was December, and cold in her draughty cell. Indira kept herself occupied by following her normal routine of getting up at five, doing yoga, reading her books and going to bed early, on a hard cot that had no mattress. Not once did she indulge in self-pity or appear depressed. 'I'll be back,' she told the Janata Party. And true to her word she was released within a week, only to emerge again as a wronged heroine.

There was no doubt now. Indira Gandhi was on a comeback trail and the Janata Party could do nothing to stop it. In any case the Janata Party alliance itself was in a state of internal disarray. With members indulging in bitter infighting there was no longer any unity among them. What had kept them together had been their one point agenda of ousting Indira Gandhi. But now with that momentum gone, the government fell and Morarji Desai was forced to resign. A former foe, Mr Charan Singh of the Syndicate, now with Indira's outside support formed the government. But Indira after a few days withdrew her support. And just thirty months after she had been forced to step down, the President announced fresh midterm elections. The year was 1980.

Indira was untiring. She criss-crossed the country campaigning hard. So fed up were the people with the petty politics of the Janata Party led alliance, they now looked upon her as a saviour. And she didn't disappoint. Promising them an effective and clean government, she won handsomely from not only Medak in Andhra Pradesh but also from Rae Bareli. Sanjay too won from Amethi.

Sworn in as prime minister for the fourth time she immediately moved back into her old house—1 Safdarjang Road—with not only Rajiv and his family but also Sanjay and his wife. In 1974 Sanjay had married Maneka, the daughter of a colonel. The wedding had been a small intimate affair at their friend Mohammad Yunus's place and Maneka had quickly adjusted to her life with the Gandhis. She was soon in the family way and within a few months of Indira's return to power, the couple had a son. He was named Varun. So Indira had a new grandson. She was happy. She had also redeemed herself in the eyes of the world and was back in the saddle once again. But there were problems galore. Insurgency was causing great instability in Assam, Nagaland, Kashmir, the Punjab and neighbouring Sri Lanka.

Phenomenal Stamina

A loving daughter, a caring mother, an affectionate grandmother, a confident globetrotter and finally prime minister in and out of office, Indira slipped into each role with ease.

While campaigning she could address twenty-five or more public meetings in thirty hours, sleep in remote bungalows, eat whatever was available and still be up with the lark. Awake, she would have a cold bath, do her yoga and hit the road for a further ten to twelve hours. She could sleep anywhere, anytime—on planes, trains or in cars; on floors, in huts or in tents. No one would guess she had been a sickly child. Her stamina and energy were remarkable.

Despite a working day of eighteen to twenty hours she would listen patiently to no less than three to five hundred people waiting to spill out their problems at her 'durbars' every day. She drew her strength from the citizens of the country.

One day she could be sitting cross-legged in silence on the floor at an ashram in Chikmaglur, the next day she could easily be in any of the world capitals, all beautifully coiffured and elegantly draped in exquisite silks, holding her own with leaders of the world. Her energy was truly amazing.

20   The Curtain Comes Down

It was 8.30 in the morning on 23 June 1980. Indira was already busy at work. Suddenly her personal assistant burst into her room. 'Something terrible has happened, madam,' he said. And as he explained Indira's world slowly crumbled around her. Sanjay was dead. Attempting some aerobic stunts with his instructor in his new Pitts S-2A two-seater plane, he had crashed near the Ridge in Delhi.

Indira rushed to the crash site. Pulled out of the wreckage, Sanjay's shattered body had already been placed in a truck. She gazed at it for a long time in anguish. Then she accompanied the body to hospital and was alone with Sanjay for some time before Maneka arrived on the scene. She was hysterical. Indira pulled herself together with an effort and sought to comfort her daughter-in-law. But Indira too was completely devastated. The loss of her mother, father and even her husband paled before the loss of her child. Soon old friends and family gathered around her. Her aunt Vijayalakshmi, who had continued to oppose her even in politics, set aside their differences and came to condole. Three months ago the family had so happily celebrated the birth of Sanjay's son Varun and now Indira was faced with the worst tragedy of her life.

The next four years were tough on Indira. Shattered and broken in spirit she began to turn to Rajiv more and more. He was a pilot with the Indian Airlines. Married in 1968 to Sonia Maino, an Italian girl whom he had met while at Cambridge, Rajiv lived a life far removed from politics. Indira, who trusted no one, wanted him to enter politics to help her. But Rajiv was not interested nor did his wife Sonia support the idea. Twenty-three-year-old Maneka was more than willing, but she was not considered old enough.

When Rajiv was persuaded to stand and win from Sanjay's constituency Amethi in 1981, Maneka was annoyed. She had expected to represent her husband's constituency. She now showed her displeasure openly. So falling out of favour with Indira, she dramatically stormed out of the Gandhi household taking her little son Varun with her. The fact that Sanjay's son was taken away from her hurt Indira deeply.

Dispirited and diffident, Indira appeared to have lost her old decisiveness. Kashmir was proving to be difficult once more. Andhra Pradesh had voted a non-Congress government to power. Karnataka brought in the Janata Party and there was violence in Assam where hundreds of Bengali refugees were massacred in a place called Nellie.

Meanwhile the situation in Punjab was also demanding urgent attention. Even though the Sikhs were given a separate state by Indira as early as 1966, many of their demands had not been met. The Akali Dal, a regional party, was fast turning into the voice of the Sikhs. Through the Anandpur Sahib Resolution it had called for, among other demands, a 'Sikh autonomous region' with its own constitution and Chandigarh as its separate capital. So to counter them and in order to split the loyalty of the Sikhs, the Congress began to prop up a certain Sant Jarnail Singh Bhindranwale. But the plan boomeranged. Bhindranwale, taking advantage of the situation, took on the mantle of a separatist leader himself and revived the demand for a sovereign state of 'Khalistan'. His followers then let loose a reign of terror in Punjab.

Every day Indira was told of fresh atrocities committed by his followers. Punjabi Hindus and Moderate Sikhs were being ruthlessly gunned down and anti-Hindu/anti-Indian speeches were inflaming tempers. Indira tried desperately to contain Bhindranwale. She tried to negotiate with him and when that failed, with the Akali Dal. But it was no use. Now when Bhindranwale, who would not have become so important but for Indira's early support, took over the Golden Temple itself and began fortifying it, the prime minister felt she had run out of options. Finally in June 1984 when the killings grew one too many with busloads of Punjabi Hindus massacred, Indira decided to send the army in. While more than half the troops that were sent in first were slaughtered, Bhindranwale was killed and the Golden Temple freed of all militants. But many innocent pilgrims too lost their lives and the Akal Takht was partially destroyed.

Operation Blue Star caused a massive uproar among the Sikhs. Beant Singh and Satwant Singh were among those who were deeply shocked. They held Indira responsible for this sacrilege and so along with a third man Kehar Singh, an ex-government employee, plotted to assassinate her. On that fateful morning on 31 October 1984, they gunned her down in cold blood. Beant Singh was killed immediately but Satwant Singh and Kehar Singh were arrested and were executed after a long trial.

Rajiv Gandhi heard the news on the BBC. He was then in West Bengal on an election tour. He returned home immediately. To avert any kind of massive reaction the party had already decided to make him prime minister. But even as he was being sworn in, the nation erupted in fury against the Sikhs. Rampaging mobs ran amuck as Indira's body lay in state in Teen Murti House awaiting cremation. It was to take three days before the army was called in to maintain peace.

Now draped in white and covered in marigolds and lilies, the cortège wound its way on the same route her father, husband and son had taken before her. Pulled by men from the three armed services, the gun carriage arrived at Shakthi Sthal on the banks of the River Jamuna where leaders from all over the world were gathered to bid her farewell. To the chanting of priests and *The Last Post* played by the army and navy buglers, a grieving Rajiv lit his mother's pyre. Thirteen days later he scattered his mother's ashes over the Himalayas she loved so much.

Thus ended the life of one of the most charismatic leaders of the world.

'My father was a statesman, I am a politician. My father was a saint, I am not . . . for most of us who grew up in the freedom struggle . . . it was not a job or a question of getting something for yourself. It was working, sacrificing and struggling for your country . . .' (*Mother India* by Pranay Gupte.)

For Indira, politics was a way of life. She had known no other.

What They Said About Her . . .

'*Sri Lanka has lost a friend whose sincerity was never in question.*'
Sirimavo Bandaranaike, prime minister of Sri Lanka.

'*My sister is dead. My sister Indira Gandhi is gone.*'
Yasser Arafat, Chairman, Palestine Liberation Organization.

'*She was a beacon for the developing world.*'
President Kenneth Kaunda of Zambia in tears.

'*An extraordinary leader and an extraordinary woman.*'
James Callaghan former British prime minister.

'*To many of us Indira Gandhi was the symbol of India. I will miss Indira Gandhi very much indeed. She was a truly great leader.*'
Margaret Thatcher prime minister of UK.

'*We slobbered over the old witch.*'
President Richard Nixon USA privately to his Secretary of State H. Kissinger after Indira's US visit in 1971.

'*Most powerful woman in the world.*'
The *Sunday Times*, UK.

21   Yet It Wasn't Always Politics

Politics may well have been Indira's way of life. And since she grew up in the shadow of the freedom struggle it may have been the only life she knew. Yet she was interested in other things. Her father had done his job well. With every letter he wrote to her, every book he made her read and every country he took her to visit, he also made her aware of a world apart from politics.

Delivering the keynote address at the UN conference on human environment in 1972, Indira spoke with authority on the need for global action to prevent nature from being destroyed in the name of progress by rich countries. She urged them not to prevent developing countries from growing on the pretext of saving the environment.

On a visit to France (1981) to receive an honorary degree from the Sorbonne University, Indira spoke to a distinguished gathering of intellectuals of the need to be a good 'global' human being. She received a standing ovation.

Indira did not have a degree nor had she finished university, yet why was she good at whatever she did? Because she prepared well. So if speeches were required

Indira read up the matter, consulted experts on the subject and used dictionaries to get the exact word she needed to convey her thoughts. She wrote and rewrote her drafts on slips of paper, cutting and pinning together various paragraphs, innumerable times, till she was personally satisfied.

And if you are wondering what she did for fun, well she managed that too. Her erratic childhood had trained her well to adjust. Hence she had acquired the knack of creating her own entertainment wherever she went. Official tours were very often converted into fun trips. She shopped at the famous Harrods (UK) or Macys (US) or Printemps in Paris where she would slip into fluent French.

In between official banquets and meetings, she would dart into a shop here or a boutique there; browse in bookshops or pick up little knick-knacks off the streets.

At home, the Central Cottage Industries on Janpath in Delhi has seen her often enough, browsing through the racks, though saris were usually sent to her to choose from.

She took off to the hills whenever possible. Almora, Nainital, Mussoorie and Simla, she loved them all, but Kashmir was always special.

She also went to plays and operas whenever she could. If it was not her favourite *Joan of Arc* in France it was *Cats* in London or even *Amadeus* in New York.

Traipsing on foot through a sleeping London, searching for a midnight snack after a poetry reading session was also no big deal for her.

Remember the story of the boy and the horse in *The Black Stallion*? She enjoyed watching it with her friends. Just like you and me.

She was equally at home with the poems of T.S. Eliot as she was with the philosophical treaties of Jiddu Krishnamurthi or Ken Follet bestsellers. She also enjoyed music, from Beethoven (classical) to Joan Baez (folk).

And she loved museums and exhibitions. On an official visit in New York, it was to the Metropolitan Museum of Arts she went to first.

She had also actually met and known many of the world's intellectuals and scientists, including Einstein and George Bernard Shaw.

Leaders across continents, Indira Gandhi knew them all personally. First, as her father's daughter and then as her own person, she was recognized and greeted as a 'very proud gracious and able lady but fiercely independent ruler with determination . . .' (*Indira Gandhi* by Pupul Jayakar).

A typical day in Indira's life:

6 a.m. Yoga-bath-breakfast-read newspaper headlines, make notes

8.30 a.m. Durbar on the lawns

10 a.m. South Block office

1 p.m. Home for lunch—a short nap—back at work

7 p.m. Home—dinner—relax a bit with friends—then work on files till midnight

In between files she could be reading out bedtime stories to her grandchildren, playing word games with them or attending to phone calls. Multitasking came easily to her.

She loved crosswords and often did them whenever she had a minute to spare. She was most offended if anyone offered her a dictionary.

Two suitcases with six khadi sarees, two large flasks of boiled water and milk, two pillows, a packet of dry fruits, peanuts and some apples accompanied her whenever she went campaigning.

Slender, quick on her feet and with a shock of white in her short black hair, she was always impeccably dressed in vibrant handlooms.

At the inauguration of the Festival of India at the Royal Festival Hall in 1982, London, the Indian national anthem was, believe it or not, in all these centuries played for the first time, in the presence of British royalty. And as the Prince of Wales and Prime Minister Margaret Thatcher stood to attention with her, Indira's eyes filled with tears of pride.

In 1983 she hosted the Commonwealth Heads of Government Meeting (CHOGM) in New Delhi. At the banquet (her last) attended by Queen Elizabeth II and other prime ministers, Indira stole the show with her resplendent silks and her regal air.

From Uzbekistan to Bastar, she also had no problem donning local costumes and keeping step to their music.

She celebrated all festivals at home and had a warm personal relationship with Anandmai, a spiritual Guru. Dhirendra Brahmachari, a tantric swami who taught her yoga, was also close to her family for a while.

She effectively used 'silence' as a weapon to show her displeasure even with leaders like the Chogyal of Sikkim, who asked her to support him against his own people, or with the Chancellor of Germany who tried to convince her not to recognize East Berlin.

She couldn't easily communicate verbally even with her family (father, husband and children). She wrote them notes instead—appreciating, criticizing or instructing.

She sued author Salman Rushdie for libel because his book *Midnight's Children* contained a reference to Sanjay, Feroze and herself which she objected to. She successfully got the reference deleted.

Always frugal, with no major wants or desires, her friends were rarely from the political world. Most of them were people she had known long.

Her friend of many years Pupul Jayakar, recalling many cosy get-togethers at Safdarjang Road and Willingdon Crescent, says she was a good and caring hostess. Often dining simply on boiled eggs and potatoes or just potluck, in or out of office, Indira would look after her guests personally. Sometimes mouth-watering pastas made by Sonia would do the rounds.

Frequently attending parent-teacher meetings as a grandmother, she mingled with other parents and children with ease—handing out sweets and eats to everyone like anybody else.

She loved having her grandchildren sleep in her bedroom. A London newspaper once referred to Indira as the only 'nappy-changing prime minister in the world'.

What would she do after retiring? 'I would like to design, just for fun . . . clothes, houses, interiors. I design my own clothes,' she said.

'Mrs Gandhi, you are such a gentle person, so caring and gracious, but no one will ever know you the way you really are,' remarked Shahnaz Hussain (Herbal Cosmetologist) once. Indira Gandhi smiled and said, 'The ones that want to know will find out for themselves.'

After Indira

Indira's son Rajiv Gandhi became prime minister by default. He was a clean and honest man who endeavoured to do a job he was not really cut out to do. His brother's death thrust him into politics and now his mother's assassination propelled him into the prime minister's office. He had wanted neither. In the elections held a few months after he became the prime minister, Rajiv won a massive mandate from the people. He remained in office for the next five years but in the 1989 elections, the Congress lost and the National Front came to power.

In 1991 it was poll time again and Rajiv was campaigning in a small town near Chennai called Sriperumbudur when a Tamil girl called Dhanu came forward to garland him. She was a suicide bomber.

Bending down to touch his feet, she detonated a bomb that blew them both to pieces. Eighteen others lost their lives that night in the blast.

Rajiv was killed for having sent the Indian Peace Keeping Force into Sri Lanka during the ethnic struggle between the Tamil and Sinhalese people in the island nation.

The Congress came back to power with P.V. Narasimha Rao as prime minister.

But 1996 to 2004 saw successive non-Congress governments.

In 1998 Rajiv's widow Sonia was pressurized into entering politics in order to help revive an ailing Congress Party. She was elected Congress President. She set to work and 2004 saw a Congress Party in coalition with other parties form a government—UPA-1. Sonia refused to become prime minister in favour of Manmohan Singh but became the Chairperson of the UPA. The 2009 elections again saw a Congress led UPA-2 come back into power. Today her two children Rahul and Priyanka continue to carry the Congress flag aloft. They are actively involved in politics.

Maneka and Varun are both Bharatiya Janata Party (BJP) MPs. They are alienated from the Congress and the rest of the Gandhi family.

TRIVIA
TREASURY

Turn the pages to discover more fascinating facts and tantalizing tidbits of history about this legendary life and her world.

WHAT HAPPENED AND WHEN

- **1917**: Birth
- **1923**: St Cecilia's Allahabad
- **1925**: L'Ecole-Internationale School Geneva
- **1926**: L'Ecole Nouvelle Bex Switzerland
- **1927**: St Mary's Convent Allahabad
- **1931**: Pupils' Own School Poona
- **1933**: Matriculation
- **1934–35**: Santiniketan
- **1935–37**: Badminton School UK
- **1937**: Sommerville College Oxford
- **1938**: Member of Indian National Congress
- **1942**: Marries Feroze Gandhi
- **1942**: Naini Jail
- **1944**: Rajiv's birth
- **1946**: Sanjay's birth
- **1948**: Nehru's Official hostess
- **1955**: Member of Congress Working Committee
- **1957**: Member of Congress Parliamentary Board
- **1959**: Member of the Indian National Congress
- **1964**: Minister of Information and Broadcasting
- **1966**: Prime Minister of India
- **1969**: Congress Splits

- **1971**: Wins elections
- **1971 (Dec)**: Fourteen Day War
- **1975 (June)**: High Court sets aside 1971 election win
- **1975 (June)**: Emergency
- **1977**: Loses election
- **1978**: 2nd Congress Split
- **1980**: Wins Election
- **1980**: Sanjay Gandhi's plane crashes
- **1984 (June)**: Operation Blue Star
- **1984 (October)**: Assassination

MEANWHILE, ELSEWHERE IN THE WORLD

- **1920**: League of Nations was established.
- **1923**: Talking movies were invented.
- **1927**: Charles Lindberg flew solo, New York to Paris, on the first transatlantic flight. Ten-year-old Indira and her father were among the cheering crowds in Paris.
- **1927**: Bubblegum was invented.
- **1931**: Empire State Building in the US was completed.
- **1939**: Helicopters were invented.
- **1945**: World's first computer–ENAIC was built.
- **1948**: Israel was founded.
- **1951**: Colour TVs were introduced.
- **1958**: Lego Toys were invented.

- **1963**: John F. Kennedy, President of USA, was assassinated.
- **1966**: *Star Trek* series was aired.
- **1969**: Neil Armstrong walked on the moon.
- **1975**: Mujibur Rahman of Bangladesh was assassinated.
- **1977**: *Star Wars* was released.
- **1979**: President Bhutto of Pakistan was executed.
- **1979**: Mother Teresa was awarded the Nobel Prize.
- **1982**: The movie *E.T.* was released.
- **1982**: Michael Jackson's *Thriller* hit the theatres.
- **1984**: Bhopal Gas Tragedy.

WHEN INDIRA SPOKE . . .

Indira disliked making speeches, but as a politician she was required to do so. Here are a few of her well-known lines:

- 'All my games were political games; I was, like Joan of Arc, perpetually being burned at the stake.'
- 'Power in itself has never attracted me, nor has position been my goal.'
- 'I cannot understand how one can be an Indian and not be proud.'
- 'My grandfather once told me that there were two kinds of people: those who do the work and those

who take the credit. He told me to try to be in the first group; there was much less competition.'
- 'You cannot shake hands with a clenched fist.'
- In 1984 just before she died, Andrew Neil of *Sunday Times* (UK) asked Indira, 'What will happen to India after you have gone?' 'India has lived a long time . . . and my sixty-six years hardly count. India will survive; will always find its feet,' she replied.

SOME AWARDS SHE WAS GIVEN

- Isabella d'Este Award (Italy) for International Relations, 1965
- Bharat Ratna, 1972
- Olympic Gold Order, 1983
- UN Population Award, 1983
- John C. Phillips Award (Spain) for Conservation of Nature, 1984
- International Lenin Peace Prize (Russia), 1985
- Jose Marti Order (Cuba), 1985
- Order of the Golden Star (Vietnam) for fighting imperialism, 1985
- Druk Wangyal (Bhutan), 1985
- Smithsonian Institute's first ever medal for outstanding service to zoological science and conservation (USA), 1986

THESE WERE HER FRIENDS . . .

In her sixty-six years Indira probably made more enemies than friends. But among those friends were:

- **Shanta Gandhi** (1919–2007)—a theatre director, dancer and playwright. Indira first met her in Pupil's Own School in Poona. The friendship continued in London where Shanta studied medicine while Indira was at Oxford. Shanta was the first person to know that Feroze and Indira were more than just friends.

- **Dorothy Norman** (1905–1997)—an American photographer, writer and social activist. Indira met her first when she went to the US with her father in 1949. The friendship survived through letters and occasional meetings till Indira's death. They went to theatres, plays and art exhibitions together whenever they could.

- **Frank Oberdorf** (1873–1894)—a young German professor who taught French to Indira in Santiniketan. The friendship was to continue till after she went to Badenweiler. He was about eighteen years older than her and is said to have been interested in her.

- **Pupul Jayakar** (1915–1997)—a doyen of art and culture. They first met in Allahabad when Indira was about fourteen and Pupul was sixteen. Her father, an Indian Civil Service (ICS) officer, was posted there. She would often go over to Anand Bhawan to play with the Nehru girls. Pupul Jayakar is largely responsible for developing the art and cultural scene in India.

- **Ralph Buultjens**—A Sri Lankan Professor of Political Science at New York University, who as a close ally helped shape Indira's ideas and decisions for many years.

FAMILY TRIVIA AND MORE

- Amitabh Bachchan met Rajiv in Allahabad when the boys were aged four and two respectively. Their mothers were friends.
- Sonia and her family stayed in Amitabh Bachchan's house in the days preceding her wedding to Rajiv as Indira did not want them to stay in a hotel. The mehendi took place there.
- A Hindi teacher was hired to teach Sonia but she preferred to learn the language on her own
- Rajiv and Sonia had two dogs—Zabul (an Afghan hound) and Reshma (a dachshund). They always fought with Sanjay and Maneka's two Irish hounds. There was also Bruno, a ferocious bull mastiff which with a Siamese cat completed the menagerie.
- When Rajiv married Sonia the bride wore the same pink and silver studded khadi saree that Indira had worn at her own wedding. Priyanka married Robert

Vadra a businessman in 1997 also clad in one of her grandmother's red and gold south Indian silks.

- Priyanka has two children, twelve-year-old Rehan and ten-year-old Miraya.
- When Maneka and Sanjay got engaged, Indira gave Maneka a turquoise and gold jewellery set and a Tanchoi saree. At the wedding Maneka also received a khadi saree which had been spun by Jawaharlal Nehru in prison. Indira herself decorated their room and chose Maneka's bangles.
- Maneka started *Surya*, a magazine which served as a mouthpiece for the family and the Congress (R) when they were out of power in 1977.
- Varun Gandhi is married to Yamini Roy. Daughter of the late diplomat Sunil Roy Chaudhary and well-known film critic Aruna Vasudev, Yamini is a graphic designer.
- Sonia worked as an art historian for a while, restoring Indian landscapes with the National Gallery of Art, New Delhi. She edited the correspondence between Indira and her father that were published as books.
- In 2011, forty years after the Bangladesh Liberation War, Sonia Gandhi went to receive the state's highest award on behalf of her mother-in-law for her contribution to the liberation.
- An Australian Director Bruce Beresford is planning to make a film on Indira Gandhi's leadership during the 1971 war.

- There is hardly a city or town in India that does not have some institution or road named after Indira. Many world capitals from Berlin, Germany ('Indira Gandhi Strabe') to Nicosia, Cyprus have named roads after her as well.
- India has brought out innumerable coins and stamps on Indira. Many other countries—USSR, Germany, Argentina, etc.—have also brought out stamps commemorating Indira.
- 1 Safdarjang Road is now a museum. It captures Indira Gandhi's life through pictures. And the place where she fell is marked out and covered in glass. Her bloodstained saree among other personal effects is also on show. Some rooms are dedicated to Rajiv Gandhi as well.
  Timings: 9.30 a.m.–5 p.m. Mondays closed.

BOOKS TO READ

Books I have read and persons who have helped while writing:

1. *Dear to Behold*, Krishna Hutheesingh (IBH Publishing Company, 1969)
2. *Indira Gandhi: A Biography*, Zareer Masani (OUP, 1978)
3. *Indira Gandhi*, Ela Sen (Rupa & Co, 1973)
4. *Discovery of India*, Jawaharlal Nehru (OUP, 2003)
5. *Indira Gandhi*, Pupul Jayakar (Penguin Books India, 1995)
6. *Mother India*, Pranay Gupte (Penguin Viking, 2009)
7. *Indira—The Life of Indira Nehru Gandhi*, Katherine Frank (Harper Collins, 2010)
8. *Letters From a Father to his Daughter*, Jawaharlal Nehru (Puffin Books India, 2004)
9. *Indira Gandhi: Courage Under Fire*, Uma Vasudev (Rupa & Co, 2003)
10. *Indira Priyadarshini*, Alaka Shankar (CBT, 1985)
11. Shri Amrit Tandon—The Jawaharlal Nehru Memorial Fund, New Delhi

Other Books in the Series

Jawaharlal Nehru: The Jewel of India
Aditi De

At midnight on 14 August 1947, Jawaharlal Nehru rose to speak to independent India as its first Prime Minister. He was dressed in a pale cream *achkan*, a white khadi cap on his head. Though his eyes had shadows beneath them, they grew brighter as Jawaharlal began to speak . . .

Pandit Nehru's words that night have remained etched in the nation's memory ever since. Born to a privileged family in Allahabad, Jawaharlal went on to become a leading figure of the Indian independence movement. During the struggle he spent over ten years in prison, watched others in his family jailed time and again, and led numerous protest marches and agitations. Working alongside Mahatma Gandhi, he helped India keep its tryst with destiny and become a free nation.

Aditi De recounts the story of Jawaharlal Nehru's extraordinary life in this sparkling biography for young readers. Filled with charming anecdotes, it recounts episodes from Nehru's childhood, and how he was drawn to the growing struggle for Indian independence. She sketches his role as the first Indian Prime Minister, and how he shaped the newly-formed democratic republic. Packed with little-known nuggets of information, and trivia about the times, this book in the *Puffin Lives* series brings alive the thoughts and actions of one of modern India's most important personalities.

Other Books in the Series

Rabindranth Tagore: The Renaissance Man
Monideepa Sahu

'The song that I came to sing remains unsung to this day. I have spent my days in stringing and in unstringing my instrument.'

—*Gitanjali*

Born in 1861 in one of the foremost families of Bengal, Little Rabi grew up to become a great nationalist, a gifted writer, a talented artist, a brilliant visionary and a reformer of education. He was also Asia's first Nobel Laureate. His contribution to India's Freedom Movement is forever immortalized in *Jana Gana Mana*, a song he wrote to inspire the nation.

This wonderfully insightful biography, rich in anecdotes and little-known facts, brings alive this legendary figure to contemporary readers. Monideepa Sahu vividly recounts Rabindranth's experiences at school that helped to formulate his vision of Shantiniketan. She also traces the evolution of his poetry from schoolboy rhymes in dog-eared notebooks to universally loved poetry, prose, novels and short stories.

Explore the life and times of this remarkable personality through this compelling biography.